I0143307

Paul's Letters to the Thessalonians 1 and 2

A Devotional Commentary

M J Flower

The St Giles Commentary Series

Grosvenor House
Publishing Limited

The right of M J Flower to be identified as the author of this
work has been asserted in accordance with Section 78
of the Copyright, Designs and Patents Act 1988

This book is published by
Grosvenor House Publishing Ltd
Link House
140 The Broadway, Tolworth, Surrey, KT6 7HT.
www.grosvenorhousepublishing.co.uk

This book is a work of fiction. Any resemblance to
people or events, past or present, is purely coincidental.

A CIP record for this book
is available from the British Library

ISBN 978-1-83615-170-8

Contents

About the Author

M J Flower, BA (Hons); MPhil, raised a family before reading Theology and Philosophy of Religion at the University of Exeter, where she also completed a research thesis on the social theory of John Millbank. She jointly established the Institute for Christian Studies in Exeter, and worked extensively with the South West Training Ministry for the Diocese of Exeter, training and supporting Readers and non-ordained ministers. She spent many years as a Churchwarden at St Leonard's Church in Exeter, and sat on the Deanery Synod as a lay member. She has spent more years than she would like to count leading and contributing to Bible Study and Home Groups and continues this work while happily retired in Buckinghamshire, living close to a very wide circle of friends and three generations of her family.

Other commentaries in the series:

The King and the Kingdom: A Devotional Commentary on the Gospel of Matthew, (London: Grosvenor House Publishing 2023)

The Acts of The Apostles: A Devotional Commentary, (London: Grosvenor House Publishing 2024)

Paul's Letter to the Galatians: A Devotional Commentary, (London: Grosvenor House Publishing 2024)

Forthcoming in 2025:

The Songs of Ascent Psalms 120-134: A Devotional Commentary.

The First Letter of Paul
to the Thessalonians

Introduction

Paul, Silas and Timothy; to the churches of the Thessalonians in God the Father and the Lord Jesus Christ. Grace to you and peace. (1 Thessalonians 1:1)

Of the twenty seven books in the New Testament, thirteen are letters sent by Paul either to Christian communities or individual Christians throughout the Roman Empire, within a few decades of the life, death and resurrection of the Lord Jesus Christ, for their instruction and encouragement.

Paul cannot be credited with writing treatises on systematic theology, though all his letters display a deep understanding of what has been revealed to him by the Holy Spirit as he has fulfilled the gift of apostleship which had been given to him. But his letters do disclose a strong desire that the emerging church should have an understanding of the glorious experience into which they have been brought through repentance towards God and faith towards our Lord Jesus Christ, (Acts 20:21); the experience of salvation; salvation from sin; liberty from bondage and slavery to the law of Moses, and the joy of being filled with the Holy Spirit as He dwells with them and is in them, according to the promise of the Lord Jesus. (John 14:17).

They are a delivered people, for those whom Jesus sets free are free indeed. (John 8:31,36).

Paul is not known by sight to all these churches. (Galatians 1:22). He also wrote to the Roman believers without having been there, though he did know some of them personally, (Romans 16:1-23), and according to the account in Acts chapter 28, he was subsequently imprisoned in Rome. But for each of these churches he had a distinctive message, according to the circumstances under which they were living out their new faith.

This is also true, of course, of his letters to the Thessalonians, which could be summarized in Paul's opening section of the letter as 'how you turned from idols to serve the living and true God; and to wait for His Son from heaven'.(1 Thessalonians 1:9,10). Taking these verses as the theme of both the Thessalonian letters gives us an understanding of the pagan society in which they lived, and from which they had been delivered; and the future hope of the Parousia, the second coming of Christ in glory to take His people to Himself and to begin the process of judgement. It is clear that Paul's preaching while in Thessalonica had had a significantly eschatological tone.

1 Thessalonians Chapter 1

1 Thessalonians 1:1. Authorship.

Paul, Silvanus and Timothy, to the church of the Thessalonians in God the Father and the Lord Jesus Christ. (1 Thessalonians 1:1).

Paul is careful to include Silvanus and Timothy in his opening words to the Thessalonians. This is not just a matter of courtesy but an acknowledgement of the valuable part played by Silas and Timothy in bringing the gospel to Thessalonica. Paul had of necessity been conducted far away from Thessalonica to Athens by 'the brethren'. This was often Paul's name for other church members, his brothers and sisters in Christ. On this occasion it was the brethren who helped him to escape the crowds of Thessalonian Jews who had been incited against him. But Silas and Timothy remained behind in Thessalonica, and no doubt the Thessalonian believers as they read these letters, would have had precious memories of the ministry of Silas and Timothy among them. (Acts 17:13,14).

The letters to the Thessalonians were among the earliest of Paul's letters, perhaps written after the one written to the Galatians, but certainly not more than twenty years after the death and resurrection of Jesus. Throughout the Roman world the gospel was already widely dispersed. It was a matter of some importance for the churches to have a written form of Christian instruction, but this was not Paul's ultimate purpose in writing to them. The believers needed encouragement; to know that they were part of God's eternal purpose in Christ; and also part of what He was doing in other towns and cities, for they had all become part of the Body of Christ.

So Paul's letters to them are full of his appreciation of them; his thanksgiving to God for them; his love for them, his brothers and sisters in Christ, and his concern that they should continue in the faith. They are very personal letters.

Paul, Silvanus (otherwise known as Silas), and Timothy, all played a significant role in Thessalonica. Paul had come to the city of Thessalonica in the province of Macedonia, northern Greece and as was his custom had preached for three Sabbaths in the synagogue, reasoning with them from the scriptures and explaining and giving evidence that the Christ, the Messiah of whom their scriptures spoke, who had suffered and risen from the dead, was *Jesus*.

Some of the Thessalonians were persuaded and joined Paul and Silas Including a number of God fearing Greeks and a number of the leading women. (Acts 17:4). But the Jews took along some wicked men who set the city in an uproar and attacked the house of Jason, searching for Paul. Not finding Paul, they dragged Jason before the city authorities, claiming that those who turned the world upside down had come to Thessalonica, 'and Jason has welcomed them'. Paul had to leave Thessalonica in a hurry to protect Jason and the other believers. (Acts 17:1-10)

The three missionaries had become separated, after having gone first to Beroea and then Paul having been escorted to Athens to escape the Jews who had discovered his whereabouts. (Acts 17:16).Then he went on to Corinth, (Acts 18:1,5), where they were reunited, and from where Paul, still comforted by these faithful brethren in spite of all the affliction he had gone through, wrote to the Thessalonians. (Bruce: *The Acts of the Apostles*. p 330). Timothy is still with him as he is writing his first letter to the Corinthians. (1 Corinthians 4:17).

The reuniting of Paul, Silas and Timothy in Corinth is a strong indication that it was from Corinth that the letter to the Thessalonians was written jointly, together, and sent to

Thessalonica. Timothy had apparently come to faith in Christ through Paul's ministry. (Acts 16:1-3). Paul calls him, 'My true child in the faith', (1 Timothy 1:2) and 'My beloved and faithful child in the Lord', (1 Corinthians 4:17).

Silvanus, sometimes abbreviated to Silas, had been a leading member of the Jerusalem church. (Acts 15:22) He had joined Paul after Paul had separated from Barnabas, (Acts 15:40), and together with Timothy and Luke, had been instrumental in bringing the gospel to Philippi, where Paul and Silas had been beaten with rods and thrown into prison, from which they had been delivered by an earthquake, after they had been singing praises to God at midnight .

Not many churches are born in an earthquake, but the church at Philippi had that distinction. The church consisted of Lydia, and the group of women who gathered together for prayer by the riverside, and a young woman who had been delivered from a spirit of divination, together with the Philppian jailer and his family. This group formed the nucleus of the Philippian church. (Acts 16:40).

Paul is insisting that there are three authors of the letter to the Thessalonians. They are collectively the 'we' of 1 Thessalonians 1:2. 'We give thanks to God always for you all'. Together, Paul, Silas and Timothy had been at the very beginning of the church in Thessalonica. Together they were concerned for the spiritual welfare of this beloved company of believers. Together they prayed for them, constantly mentioning them in their prayers, (1 Thessalonians 1:2). Together, they remembered 'before our God and Father, your works of faith and labour of love and steadfastness of hope in our Lord Jesus Christ, (1 Thessalonians 1:3).

Only at the end of the letter after Paul had requested that the Thessalonians pray for them too, does he add, '*I* adjure you by the Lord Jesus that this letter be read by all the brethren',

(1 Thessalonians 5:27), perhaps indicating that this letter, or copies of it, could be shared with other churches in Macedonia, but also suggesting that what is written in the letter is his responsibility as far as its legitimacy is concerned; that its content is revealed truth; though not detracting from any contributions made by Silas or Timothy, but only, as it were, setting a seal upon it.

Though both Silas and Timothy are absolutely one with Paul in this ministry, it appears that when comparing the content of this letter with others which Paul sent to other churches, there had been some who had suggested that there was a question mark over the authenticity of Paul's apostleship. It is important that through this letter, the believers in Thessalonica are able to understand that Paul is seen to be what he elsewhere describes himself to be; an apostle sent by God, (Romans 1:1), and that therefore, the gospel which he had preached was totally authentic. The Thessalonian believers need have no doubt about the authority of what had been written to them. *God* had sent him to them, and now he was writing to them. Paul's *intense concern* for his readers *accounts also* for the similarity of style and content of this letter to others. (1 Thessalonians 2:7,11). The letter was from them all, from Paul and Silas and Timothy, but the author was Paul. (Bruce, *Word Bible Commentary* pp xx, xxi).

1 Thessalonians 1:1. The gospel comes to Macedonia.

Paul, Silvanus and Timothy, to the church of the Thessalonians, in God the Father and the Lord Jesus Christ.

Macedonia became a province of Rome after an uprising in 148 B.C., by an adventurer called Andriscus. Then, to ensure security in the province, the Romans built a highway through Macedonia, northern Greece, called the Via Egnatia, from Apollonia on the Adriatic coast to Thessalonica, then on to Phillipi and Neapolis, and later extended to Byzantium, modern Constantinople. (Bruce, *Word Bible Commentary* p xx).

Macedonia, northern Greece, thus became a centre for the exercise of Roman power and authority, in combination with Achaia, southern Greece; and Thessalonica became the seat of provincial administration. It was an important city, the largest and most important in Macedonia, situated as it was, halfway between the Adriatic Sea and the Hellespont, at the entrance to the Black Sea. It had a fine harbour, and being at the central point where many roads met, had made it wealthy, with the trade and merchandise of a trade route passing through it. The Via Egnatia, the Roman gateway from Rome to the east, went through its centre.

There were of course many Roman residents in the city, but it remained substantially Greek. It also had a flourishing Jewish community.

After the Council of Jerusalem (Acts 15:5-29), Paul and Silas set out from Jerusalem, ostensibly to take the Jerusalem decree to the infant churches so recently established. They went from Jerusalem through to Syria, crossed the sea to Cilicia and came to Derbe and Lystra in Asia Minor where Timothy joined them, through part of Galatia where they were forbidden to speak the word by the Holy Spirit, (Acts 16:6), and continued northwards. They attempted to go into Bithynia but the Spirit of Jesus did not allow them. (Acts 16:7), so passing by Mysia, they went down to Troas, on the west coast of the Adriatic Sea at the northernmost limit of Asia Minor. Bruce conjectures that as far as can be inferred, they were making for Ephesus. (Bruce, *Word Bible Commentary* p xx).

But at Troas, Paul had a vision in the night, a man of Macedonia standing and beseeching, 'Come over into Macedonia and help us'. (Acts 16:9). Now joined by Luke, the four men immediately sought to go on into Macedonia, 'concluding that God had called us to preach the gospel to them'. (Acts 16:10). They set sail from Troas and made for Samothrace, and the next day to the port of Neapolis about ten miles from Philippi. The Via

Egnatia reached the sea after passing through Thessalonica, Amphipolis and Philippi.

After Paul and Silas had suffered extreme treatment at the hands of the authorities in Philippi, and had established a small Christian community there, they continued their journey westward, along the Via Egnatia, for ninety miles, until they came to Thessalonica. (Acts 17:1). Stott comments that Paul, Silas, Timothy and Luke were the four missionaries who had sailed across the Aegean Sea from Asia into Europe, taking the gospel into Europe. (Stott p 17).

It appears that Paul had a policy of 'to the Jews first and also to the Greeks', (Romans 1:16), for in every place to which he went, his first objective was always the preaching of the gospel in the synagogue. Paul now found a synagogue of the Jews in Thessalonica and for three weeks, as was his custom, argued with them from the Hebrew scriptures. (Acts 17:1,2). His message was serious, that the Messiah of whom their scriptures spoke was Jesus. This they might possibly have accepted. But he went on to say that this Jesus, whom he declared to be the Messiah, had been crucified and had risen from the dead. Their scriptures spoke of many cruel and inhumane ways in which someone could be put to death, but at that time the method of death by crucifixion had not yet been imported to Macedonia from Rome.

It was true that there were passages lin their scriptures like those in Isaiah which spoke of the Suffering Servant, the One who was despised and rejected of men, a man of sorrows and acquainted with grief, who was wounded for their transgressions and bruised for their iniquities, (Isaiah 53:3,5). But the cross? Their scriptures also spoke of anyone being hanged on a tree as being accursed of God. (Deuteronomy 21:23). And Paul is also emphatic that Jesus rose from the dead.

These two aspects of Paul's teaching about the Messiah were very difficult for Jews. Paul said to them: 'this Jesus whom

I preach to you is the Christ, the Messiah'. (Acts 17:3). Paul was explaining and proving to the Thessalonians that it was necessary for the Christ to suffer and to rise from the dead. (Acts 17:3). Could they believe that the scriptures foretold a Messiah who would suffer in this way? Or that if someone called Jesus had been crucified, He was now alive having risen from the dead? And had been exalted to the right hand of God His Father in heaven?

But it seems that in every synagogue to which Paul went, there were some who joyfully received his message of salvation from sin through this crucified one, who were persuaded of this amazing truth. (Acts 17:4). This was the case in Thessalonica, and many Jewish people, along with a large number of the God-fearing Greeks and a number of the leading women, joined Paul and Silas. (Acts 17:4).

This augmentation of the numbers of people who were becoming believers, especially outright pagans who were being converted, many of whom had turned to God from idols to serve the living and true God, (1 Thessalonians 1:9,10), posed a serious threat; a serious assault on the beliefs, customs and traditions of conservative Jews. The number of Jews who were being persuaded by Paul that Jesus was indeed the Messiah, and that He fulfilled all the prophecies of scripture, was also a threat to the continuation of the synagogue. The Jews were jealous, (Acts 17:5), and greatly disturbed.

Bruce reminds us, (p xxiii) that it was just about this time, 49 A.D., that the emperor Claudius had expelled the Jews from Rome, including Aquila and Priscilla, (Acts 18:2), so the Jews were probably in siege mode, sensitive to any kind of perceived militancy which would jeopardize the privileged position which the Jews had, until recently, enjoyed.

The Jews engaged 'some lewd fellows of the baser sort', (Acts 17:5. K.J.V.); some 'wicked fellows of the rabble' (R.S.V), to instigate a riot in the city, to set the city in an uproar. This was a mistake. It was because of the persistent rioting of the Jews that Claudius had expelled them from Rome and there would be heavy penalties after this riot, including the persecution of those who had become Christians, who had come to be regarded by the authorities as a Jewish sect. (1 Thessalonians 2:14)

Unable to lay hands on Paul, the rioters attacked the house of Jason, who perhaps was one of those who had been 'persuaded' by Paul, (Acts 17:4), and in whose house Paul was staying; but not finding Paul, they dragged Jason before the city authorities, crying,'These men who have turned the world upside down have come here also, and Jason has received them. And they are acting against the decrees of Caesar, saying, there is another king, Jesus'. (Acts 17:6).

They are thus accusing Paul and his companions of sedition, setting up Jesus as an alternative emperor or ruler. Paul had indeed claimed the Lordship of Christ, that the Messiah foretold in the scriptures would come again to the earth to be the Judge of all people, the Lord Jesus revealed from heaven with His mighty angels in flame of fire, inflicting vengeance on those who do not know God and upon those who who do not obey the gospel of Jesus. (2 Thessalonians 1:7,8). There was undoubtedly an apocalyptic thread running through Paul's preaching to them. The city authorities were disturbed when they heard this, that there was another king, King Jesus, (Acts 17;8). Concerned that their own allegiance to Rome could be called into question, they contented themselves with making Jason responsible for his friend's good behaviour, and let them go. (Acts 17:9).

Paul, Silas and Timothy could not stay in Thessalonica under those conditions, for it put Jason and the emerging church at risk. Though he had been with them for such a short time, Paul envisaged that the new believers, encouraged by their new faith, would be going through quite a period of opposition after he had left them, and according to 2 Thessalonians 1:4, this proved to be the case. Paul writes of their 'steadfastness and faith in all your persecutions and in all the afflictions which you are enduring'.

Jason, together with Sosipater of Beroea and Timothy, are mentioned in Romans 16:21 and in Acts 20:4, and also Aristarchus and Secundus of the Thessalonians, describing them as steadfast men of faith, fellow workers with Paul. And though Paul writes that he had wanted to come to them time and again, but had been hindered, (1 Thessalonians 2:18), he later had an opportunity to return through Macedonia, and had gone through those parts, and given them much encouragement. (Acts 20:1,2)

We may also assume that Paul had been able to visit the believers in Thessalonica as he went through Macedonia on the return journey from Corinth, to Troas and Phillipi, where he had spent three months. (Acts 20, 2-5).

This of course was later. Paul and Silas had quietly left Thessalonica by night and, escorted by the brethren, came to Beroea, some way north of the Via Egnatia. As was Paul's custom, he went into the Jewish synagogue to preach the gospel. Beroea was the home of Sosipater. As in Thessalonica those who became believers included several Greek women of high standing, as well as men, who received the word with all eagerness, searching the scriptures daily to see if these things were so. And many of them therefore, believed. (Acts 17:11, 12)

But his productive time in Beroea was interrupted by Jews from Thessalonica, who, having learned that Paul was proclaiming the word of God in Beroea, came there too, stirring up the crowds.

Once again, Paul had to be relocated, though Silas and Timothy remained in Beroea. The Beroean believers, (for there was now a Christian community in Beroea), brought Paul as far as Athens, from where Paul sent a message to Silas and Timothy, asking them to join him as soon as possible, (Acts 17:14), which they did, according to 1 Thessalonians 3:1. Paul then sent Timothy to Thessalonica and sent Silas elsewhere in Macedonia, possibly Phillipi. (Acts 18:5; 1 Thessalonians 3:6). And from Corinth, Paul writes his letters to the Thessalonians. (Bruce. *The Acts of the Apostles* p 330).

This had been the foray of the four friends, including Luke, into Europe. Apart from Paul's time in Beroea, they had met with opposition, persecution, beatings and imprisonment. Because of this persecution they had been compelled to leave one Macedonian city after another. Had Paul been mistaken about the vision of the man from Macedonia, pleading with him to 'come over to Macedonia and help us'? (Acts 16:9). Surely the answer lies in the fact that in all those cities there was now a community of believers. It was just a nagging concern of Paul's that these infant Christians had not been given enough instruction and encouragement, especially in the face of what could be ongoing opposition.

His concern was commendable and admirable and because of it he wrote these precious letters which are so valuable to us today. But in reality, his concern was unwarranted. Both he and his beloved Thessalonian believers were constantly being given the grace of God, and the peace which comes from trusting Him. Of this wonderful grace and peace Paul reminds them both at the beginning and end of each letter. Morris helpfully explains that grace, *charis, (Gk),* fundamentally means that which causes joy, *charein, (Gk),* which includes *chara,* from *charein to charis,* and comes to mean God's kindness in providing for the spiritual needs of believers, His free gift of grace; His favour towards us. (Morris p 37). God's grace, God's joy.

With the exception of Galatians, where the Galatian believers have to wait for a while before Paul assures them of God's grace towards them, (Galatians 1:3), all Paul's letters begin with grace.

14

There is safety, security, joy and unstinting love and protection for all who have come to the knowledge and love of God, the grace of the Lord Jesus Christ. 'Grace to you and peace'. (1 Thessalonians 1:1).

1 Thessalonians 1:1. The church of God in Thessalonica.

Paul, Silvanus and Timothy, to the church of the Thessalonians in God the Father and the Lord Jesus Christ. Grace to you and peace. (1 Thessalonians 1:1).

From the outset of this letter, Paul is writing to the Thessalonians that their church is *in God,* incorporated into Him, that He is the true sphere in which the church exists. Paul adds, 'and *in* the Lord Jesus Christ', including the Lord Jesus Christ under the same preposition. This at one and the same time bears witness to the exaltation of Christ and points to the participation of the believers in the risen life of Christ. He is the Lord Jesus Christ and they are members of His Body, the church. They are the *ekklesia, (Gk),* the 'called out' ones, the 'gathered out' ones, both Jews and Gentiles, without distinction.

Paul's greeting to them has been, 'grace and peace to you'. Lightfoot comments, *Grace, charis Gk, is the source of all blessing, eirene,Gk, peace, their end and issue.* (J.B.Lightfoot. *St. Paul's Epistles to the Ephesians, to the Colossians and Philemon.* p 134. Macmillan 1884. Quoted by Stott, p 30).

This letter was sent to the Thessalonians and was received by them only a few weeks or at the most, months, after Paul, Silas and Timothy had left the city. They were in need of both grace and peace as they faithfully continued to serve the living and true God and wait for His Son from heaven. (1 Thessalonians 1:9,10). Grace and peace are not just an introductory formula. Paul has a real desire in his heart, that as they had begun so well, so they would continue, and they will need the grace of God and the Lord Jesus Christ to enable them, and to impart to them the precious gift of His peace.

Paul begins by affirming them. He writes, 'We, Paul, Silvanus and Timothy give thanks to God always for you all', and then, assuring them of this, goes on to say that 'we are constantly remembering you in our prayers, mentioning you before our God and Father. (1 Thessalonians 1:2).

While these men of faith, men of God, would have spent time in private prayer, it is inconceivable that they would not have spent time in prayer together. This is in itself an encouragement to the believers in Thessalonica, to know that these men who had so faithfully brought the gospel to them were constantly praying for them, 'remembering before our God and Father your work of faith and labour of love and steadfastness of hope in our Lord Jesus Christ. (1 Thessalonians 1:3).

There is here again, as in so many of Paul's letters, the triad of faith, hope and love. (1 Thessalonians 5:8; Romans 5:1-5; 1 Corinthians 13:12; Galatians 5:5; Colossians 1:4; Ephesians 4:2-5); faith as the gateway to the knowledge of sins forgiven; love as the comforting relationship with our own Heavenly Father; hope that one day we shall see the risen Christ in all His glory; and that until that day comes, 'He who began a good work in us will complete it until the day of Jesus Christ'.(Philippians 1:6).

Paul gives much value to thanksgiving. It is a constituent of his own life and he recommends it to his many friends and fellow Christians as a sure way of recognizing the hand of God over his and their lives. And when faced with adversity, he suggests that 'in everything, by prayer and supplication, *with thanksgiving,* let your requests be made known to God'. (Phillipians 4:6). And he is constantly thanking God for his brothers and sisters in Christ. (1 Corinthians 1:4; Philippians 1:3; Colossians 1:3; Romans 1:8; Ephesians 1:16).

Writing to the Thessalonians, he thanks God for their works of faith and labour of love and steadfastness of hope in our Lord

Jesus Christ.This may ring alarm bells for us. What does Paul mean by 'works of faith', when we consider what James has to say about faith without works being dead?.

Martin Luther, that great man of the Reformation, was concerned about the disjunction between salvation by faith alone, and those who sought to earn their way to salvation by works which they had done, supposedly using James' principle that without works, faith is dead. On this reading, or interpretation of James' letter, Luther called it 'an epistle of straw'. (Wanamaker p 75).

But this is surely not what James intended. His concern was that believers should show by their works, that that faith, through which they received salvation, issues in a life of faith, and produces works of faith in the life of a follower of Jesus.

In substance, Paul's concern is not very different from that of James. He is convinced that it is impossible by works that we have done, to earn our way into salvation.To the Galatians he writes that a man is not justified, made righteous and fit to stand before a holy God, by works of the law, but *only* by faith in Christ.. He continues that if justification were by the law, obtained through some kind of obedience to the law which gave men and women a sense of self achievement, then Christ died in vain, unnecessarily. It is only through the cross of Christ that we find redemption, and justification, not by works that we have done, but by His gift of faith by which we are set free from the law; faith in the atoning work of Christ on the cross to bear away our sin, being given the righteousness of Christ, being justified by faith in Him.

Paul is writing to the Galatians of the *outcome of faith,* its purpose, in works that are characteristic of the life of faith. It is the work that is produced by faith, that springs from faith. Morris says, 'Theirs was no barren assent to the dogma of James 2::17, but the dynamic outworking of a life transforming principle, that of Galatians 5:6, faith working through love'. (Morris p 39).

Stott comments, Paul usually emphasises the faith which issues *in* works, and James the works that issue *from* faith. (James 2:18; Stott p.30).

Paul also remembers the 'labour of love' of the Tessalonians (1 Thessalonians 1:3). This phrase is sometimes used of a task, inconvenient or tiresome, which is performed without thanks or reward. It is not what Paul means by a labour of love. He knows that the Thessalonians have sometimes laboured to the point of weariness or exhaustion, activated by love for a person or persons; *agape* love which comes from God and is a reflection of His great love for us. (1 John 4:10). In this is love, not that we loved God but that He loved us, and gave His Son to be the propitiation, the atoning sacrifice for our sins. If we have not known this love, John says, we have not known God.

As these believers wait for His Son from heaven, (1 Thessalonians 1:9,10), they build one another up in love. They care for one another and they care for others who have not yet come to faith, those who are not yet part of the *ekklesia*, the Body of Christ.

Love is not just an emotion, but a working together, a labour, an activating force, witnessing to the tremendous life transforming experience of becoming a child of God. And Paul does not stop there. He tells the Thessalonian believers that he remembers their steadfastness of hope in our Lord Jesus Christ. Throughout Paul's letters, hope is described as something powerful. It is not just wishful thinking or optimism, or having a happy disposition. For the Thessalonian believers, and for believers everywhere it is a sure conviction that what God has promised, He is able also to perform. (Romans 4:21).

But crucially, the Thessalonian believers are not 'as those who have no hope, for they believe that since Jesus died and rose again, even so will God bring with Him those who have fallen asleep, at the coming of the Lord. (1 Thessalonians 4:13,14). They steadfastly believe in the coming of His Son from heaven.

(1 Thessalonians 1:10). Their hope is in the expectation of their Lord's soon returning to take His power and reign, and this leads to their steadfastness of hope, their endurance in the face of opposition. (1 Thessalonians 2:14). Their steadfastness is the result of that hope, for they know that God is in control.

The faith, hope and love of the Thessalonians is what Paul remembers about them, and he remembers it as he prays for them, remembering them before our God and Father and the Lord Jesus Christ. And as he prays for them, he gives thanks for them.

1 Thessalonians 1:2-5. Chosen of God.

We give thanks to God for you all, knowing brethren beloved of God, that He has chosen you. For our gospel did not come to you in word only, but also in power and in the Holy Spirit, and with full conviction. (1 Thessalonians 1:2-5).

Paul also gives thanks for them because they are brethren beloved of God; that He had chosen them. Paul often calls believers 'brethren', the word being a generic term which includes brothers and sisters. He calls them brethren because he wants to remind them of their relationship to each other as well as to the Lord Jesus Christ. They are family, brothers and sisters. They may call God 'Father', and know themselves to be His adopted children; (Romans 8:29), His adopted 'sons', (also generic, meaning 'sons *and* daughters'). They have a new social and familial identity. Paul calls them 'brethren beloved of God' which summarizes all their newfound relationships as they have come to faith, what Wanamaker calls, 'the language of belonging'. (Wanamaker p 77).

This aspect, the aspect of belonging arises from the reality that God has chosen them. This introduces the whole subject of election. It is obvious to other believers that these men and women are chosen by God because of the evidence of their lives;

their works of faith; their labour of love; their steadfastness of hope in our Lord Jesus Christ.

But they were not chosen by God because of these evidences, which were of course evidence of the work of the Holy Spirit in their lives. God's choosing of them was 'according to the purpose of Him who accomplishes all things according to the counsel of His will'. (Ephesians 1:11). Those who first trusted in Christ have been *destined, and appointed to live for the praise of His glory. (Ephesians 1:12).*

Paul, Silas and Timothy had gone to Thessalonica preaching the word, and the Thessalonians had received the word in much affliction, but also with joy inspired by the Holy Spirit, for the word of the gospel which came to them came not only in word, but also in power and in the Holy Spirit and with full conviction, the *pleroma, (Gk),* the fullness of conviction. (1 Thessalonians 1:5,6).

It may be that in Thessalonica, as in Galatia, (Galatians 3:5), the Holy Spirit had manifested His power in miracles among them. But Paul gives no explanation as to why God should have chosen these men and women and not others. They are lovers of God and chosen by God. The mystery for them is that God should love them so much that He has chosen them to be the recipients of His grace. They knew that they were unworthy of such love, the love revealed in Jesus and what He had done on the cross; such costly love; but He had held out His arms to them and they had run into them and learned to call Him Father.

Perhaps He had held out His arms to others and they had rejected Him, and He knew in His omniscience that this would be so, yet continued to show them His love. But even though they were beginning to understand the love of God, revealed in all its terrifying cosmic power on the cross, their election did not depend on their acceptance or rejection of such great love, but was dependent on the eternal will of God, for they were chosen in Him from before the foundation of the world. (Ephesians 1:4). And He has never altered or changed His plan, HIs eternal purpose.

If they had imagined that some sudden whim of theirs had decided their whole eternal destiny, they were mistaken. Their election rests on the solid ground of God's predetermined thought concerning them. The Lord knows those who are His. (2 Timothy 2:19), and though they may never understand fully why not all are called, this statement of Paul's to Timothy is a firm foundation under their feet. It is clearly God's inerrant choice. We have no choice but to rest in His wisdom and His unfailing love. It is our privilege, and not our right, to know that we are secure and safe, by His grace, safe in His choice and determined that as far as we are able, we will, as Paul did, proclaim the gospel wherever we can, for there may well be others who have not yet understood their destiny in Christ.

Election is what makes the 'called out ' ones the *ekklesia*, (Karl P. Donfried p 30), called *out* from among the citizens of Thessalonica, and called *into* the kingdom of heaven. This calling out is the impetus, the motivation behind their work of faith, labour of love and steadfastness of hope in the Lord Jesus Christ.

1 Thessalonians 1:5-7. Paul's ministry in Thessalonica.

For our gospel came to you not only in word, but also in power and in the Holy Spirit and with full conviction.You know what kind of men we proved to be among you for your sake. And you became imitators of us and the Lord, for you received the word in much affliction, with joy inspired by the Holy Spirit. So that you became an example to all the believers in Macedonia and Achaia.(1 Thessalonians 1:5-7).

Paul says, '*our*' gospel came to you, obviously including Silas and Timothy In the proclamation of the good news of sins forgiven and peace with God; of justification, being made righteous by faith; of access to grace and joy in hope of sharing the glory of God. (Romans 5:1-2). This was the gospel which these three men of God wanted to share with them.

These could have been just words, ideas, aspirations. But they were not just propositions. They needed the power of God and the Holy Spirit to make them real, to give them substance and reality and verity. (1 Thessalonians 1:5). And this power was devolved to Paul, Silas and Timothy by the Holy Spirit. Though Paul speaks of 'our'gospel, it did not belong to them as though it was their ability to put together words and sentences in such a way that people were persuaded into believing. The gospel was entrusted to them as a precious gift to be shared with others, that they too might enjoy the glory of God, the Holy Spirit bearing witness to the word, the good news, the glad tidings of the gospel being preached in 'the fulness of conviction', (1 Thessalonians 1:5), emphasising that there was no room for anything else; no room for doubt or compromise.

The Thessalonian believers were fully convinced, fully persuaded of the truth of the gospel. It was totally satisfying to their minds and to their hearts and could not be gainsaid. It was full and blessed assurance, a foretaste of glory divine as they willingly submitted themselves to the will of God for their lives. They were happy and blessed, rejoicing in the Holy Spirit, so that they became an example to all the believers in Macedonia and Achaia, (1 Thessalonians 1:7), Macedonia in the north, and Achaia in the south, of Greece.

The Thessalonian believers had seen this contentment in Paul, and Silas and Timothy, as they walked in faith, doing the will of God. These were the kind of men the missionaries were and proved to be as they lived among them, (1 Thessalonians 1:5). And they lived this way for the sake of those people to whom they had come with the gospel. It was almost inevitable that the Thessalonian believers should become 'imitators of them and of the Lord'. (1 Thessalonians 1:6), for He too led a contented life, completely trusting in His heavenly Father.

1 Thessalonians 1:8. The faith of the Thessalonians.

For the word of the Lord has sounded forth from you, not only in Macedonia and Achaia, but also in every place your faith in God has gone forth, so that we have no need to say anything, (1 Thessalonians 1:8).

The Thessalonians had received the word in much affliction. It had not been an easy time. But they also received the word with joy inspired by the Holy Spirit as they became imitators of Paul, Silas and Timothy; and other believers in Macedonia and Achaia, both northern and southern Greece, and became imitators of them. (1 Thessalonians 1:6,7).

For the word of the Lord had sounded out from among the Thessalonians; in every place their faith in God had gone forth, so that Paul, Silas and Timothy did not need to say anything about them and the welcome they received, except that they had turned from idols to serve the living and true God and to wait for His Son from heaven.

It seemed that all Macedonia and Achaia had been aware of the tremendous happenings in Thessalonica, but in this letter, Paul was not concentrating on the opposition and rioting that had happened, with all the city in an uproar, (Acts 17:5), but on the message which he brought them, the message that it was necessary for the Christ to suffer and to rise from the dead, saying to them, 'This Jesus whom I preach to you, is the Christ' (Acts 17:3)

What was so much more significant to him than the civil unrest, was what had transpired in the lives of men and women who had believed his report, had turned to Christ and were living joyful lives, rejoicing in the power of the Holy Spirit and their new status as children in the family of God, waiting for His Son from heaven whom He raised from the dead, Jesus who delivers us from the wrath to come, (1 Thessalonians 1:10).

Even as the preaching of the word to them had been in the power of the Holy Spirit, so they understood their own need to rely on Him as He led them into relationship with Him. Even their suffering, which probably increased after Paul had been compelled to leave them, (Acts 17:9), gave them joy, for they knew they were walking in the footsteps of their Lord who had also suffered.

They may even have heard of the experiences of others, like Peter and John who rejoiced that they were counted worthy to suffer for the sake of the Name. (Acts 5:41). Paul himself later wrote that above everything else, he wanted to know Christ and the power of His resurrection, and to share in His sufferings. (Phillipians 3:10). Dr Morris remarks that all our values are transformed by the power of God's Holy Spirit when we enter into the salvation bought for us at the tremendous cost of the blood of Christ. (Morris p 49).

It was their faith in God which had gone forth everywhere. (1 Thessalonians 1:8). They are believers, not social workers, and their faith was sounded forth in evangelism, sharing the word of God with others throughout Macedonia and Achaia, present day Greece. We remember their strategic geographical positioning on the Via Egnatia, facilitating the going forth of the gospel 'everywhere'.

There is much emphasis these days on good works, works of charity, works of social significance being performed by church members and rightly so, for Christians should never be blind to the needs of others. Loving our neighbour is the second of the two greatest commandments; firstly to love God, and then to love our neighbour as ourselves. (Deuteronomy 6:5; Leviticus 19:18; Luke 10:27). Later, we read of the extreme poverty of the churches of Macedonia, including Thessalonica, which nevertheless overflowed in the wealth of their liberality, begging Paul to allow them to participate in the support of the saints in Jerusalem. (2 Corinthians 8:1-4; Romans 15:26).

But their priority was the message of the cross. They had turned from idols to serve the living and true God and to wait for His Son from heaven, whom He raised from the dead, that is, Jesus, who delivers us from the wrath to come. (1 Thessalonians 1:9,10).

This was a serious commitment on their part. It was a pagan environment in which they lived and much of it was very beautiful. The Greeks had many beautiful statues of the gods; they had the Acropolis in Corinth, and the Areopagus or Mars Hill for the worship of the god of war in Athens. There were many beautiful shrines to the gods, for it was a polytheistic society. But their gods had no reality behind them, except that of producing, and promoting fear and a need to appease these figures of their own creation induced by 'the elemental spirits of the universe'. (Galatians 4:3,9).

In 1 Corinthians 8:4, Paul writes that an idol has no real existence, that there is no god but One. For though there may be so called gods in heaven and earth, as indeed there are, many gods and many lords, yet there is only one God, the Father, *from* whom are all things, and for whom we exist, and one Lord, Jesus Christ *through* whom are all things and for whom we exist .

God alone is real, living and true. He alone is truth, is reality, even as Jesus claimed for Himself, 'I am the way, *and the truth* and the life. No one comes to the Father except through Me. (John 14:6).

Paul describes this as 'the present evil age', (Galatians 1:4), and the Galatian believers, before they came to faith, as 'slaves to the elemental spirits of the universe'. from whom the Galatians had turned to the knowledge of God. (Galatians 4:3). The same could be said of the Thessalonians. Paul also notes that that which is offered to idols is actually offered to demons. (1 Corinthians 10:20). Like the Corinthians too, the Thessalonians had also served idols, but now they had turned from idols to serve the living and true God. They had been 'slaves ' to idols. Now they had become 'slaves' to God.

Idols are false gods, but they may have a tremendous hold on people's minds and hearts. Stott speaks of tribes that are animistic, often today called tribal religions, where people live in superstitious dread of them. (Stott p 39). And the very thought of breaking away from them fills them with alarm as they fear the spirit's revenge, says Stott.

But whether primitive or sophisticated, to turn away from what has formed a sense of spiritual security, something which is tangible and visible, to a God who is invisible, intangible, requires more than just the courage of separation from all that a person has previously known and believed. It requires that the gospel carries with it the power of God unto salvation, (Romans 1:16). The power of God was much in evidence among the people of Thessalonica, turning them from the worship of false and dead idols to the living God, granting them courage and resolution, and ever increasing joy.

1 Thessalonians 1:9,10. The coming KIng.

> For they themselves report about the kind of reception we had with you, and how you turned to God from idols to serve a living God, and to wait for His Son from heaven, Jesus, who delivers us from the wrath to come. (1 Thessalonians 1:9,10).

These Thessalonians have begun a new life in Christ. They had turned away from an old slavery to a new slavery. They have become slaves, servants of the Lord Jesus Christ, 'whose service is perfect freedom'. (Book of Common Prayer. The collect for peace *and concord).* They have turned from idols to serve a living and true God and wait for His Son from heaven. They have a new focus, a new purpose for their lives, a new future as they wait for the Lord Jesus to descend from heaven.

This is the apocalyptic thread running throughout 1 and 2 Thessalonians, that God has a further purpose in view. He has already exalted His Son to His right hand. He says to His beloved One, 'Sit at My right hand until I make Your enemies a footstool for your feet.' (Psalm 110:1). And there is a future time coming when He will come again, a second time, to this earth and to the people whom He loves and for whom He died; that He might take them home with Him, to the glory which He shares with His Father, and to dwell with Him forever.

This is their hope, the hope of the coming end of time and future glory, when they will dwell in His presence, where those who love Him will see His face, not in a glass darkly or in a mirror dimly, but they will know fully, even as they have been fully known. (1 Corinthians 13:12; Revelation 22:4). This is His promise to them. This is sufficient motivation for whatever He asks them to do for Him, even if it involves suffering for His sake. He will come again for them and they will be delivered from the wrath to come, the judgement of God on all those who have mocked him and put Him to an open shame, dishonouring Him, holding Him up to contempt. (Hebrews 6:6. K.J.V; R.S.V).

How could the Thessalonians cease from sharing the gospel as they pondered these amazing truths? That the future would be glorious for those who believe was an amazing revelation. But they knew of many who would be subject to the wrath of God; and His sorrow as He turned His face away from them saying, 'I never knew you. Depart from Me'. (Matthew 7::23). How serious would His judgement be when He came again. So those waiting from His Son from heaven were not sitting idly with their hands folded, sure of their future destiny, but were full of a desire to sound forth the word of the Lord throughout Macedonia and

Achaia, and not only in the immediate vicinity, but 'everywhere', that others might enjoy the privilege of coming to faith and finding new life in Christ. (1 Thessalonians 1:8). They were indeed imitators of those who had gone this way before them, even to the extent of suffering for their faith as Paul now reminds them.

1 Thessalonians Chapter 2

1 Thessalonians 2: 1-12. Principles of evangelism.

For you yourselves know, brethren, that our visit to you was not in vain, but though we had already suffered and been shamefully treated at Philippi, as you know, we had courage in our God to declare to you the gospel of God in the face of great opposition. (1 Thessalonians 2:1-2).

It appears from 1 Thessalonians 2:2 that the first requirement for preachers of the gospel is courage. Although Paul and Silas had been shamefully treated at Philippi, as the Thessalonians knew, they did not allow their brutal treatment to discourage them from preaching the gospel when they came to Thessalonica. They preached the gospel of God in the face of great opposition. (1 Thessalonians 2:2).

Paul acknowledges that it is possible to preach the gospel out of error, or uncleanness, or with deceitfulness or guile. (1 Thessalonians 2:3). But this so-called but false gospel is preached not to please God but to please men, and is altogether worthless because it often uses words of flattery or is a cloak for greed, bringing people into condemnation or into a false sense of spiritual security.

From 1 Thessalonians 2:3, Stott assumes that Paul and Silas had been accused of preaching the gospel in this way. (Stott p 46). But Paul says that it was not the way he and Silas preached the gospel. They had only sought the approval of God and were all the time conscious that their hearts, their motivation, was being tested by Him. (1 Thessalonians 2:4).

Though it is possible that the conduct or motives of Paul and his companions had been represented in an unfavourable light, they knew that only if they conducted themselves in a manner worthy of the gospel (Philippians 1:27), could they expect new believers to do the same; that they could confidently expect the Thessalonians to be imitators of them. (1 Thessalonians 1:6. Bruce p 27).

And Paul has another reason for preaching the gospel worthily. He believes that the gospel was given to him as a sacred trust and must only be preached to please God and not men. (1 Thessalonians 2:6).For this reason, although they were apostles of Christ, Paul and Silas made no demands on the Thessalonians, even though they may have been entitled to do so, On the contrary, they were gentle among them, like a nursing mother taking care of her children, because they were 'affectionately desirous of them'. (1 Thessalonians 2:7).

Their love for the Thessalonians had become so great that only their reception of the gospel and their walk of faith could satisfy the desires of the apostles towards them. The desire of the hearts of the apostles was that they should be permitted to share with the Thessalonian believers, not their material belongings, but their own selves, 'because they had become very dear to them'. (1 Thessalonians 2:9).

This was the extent of their love for them. The apostles were ready to share not only the gospel with them but also their own selves.

The only thing that they would not share with them was the burden of their daily living, on the principle that children ought not to lay up for their parents but parents for their children. (2 Corinthians 12:14), Paul reminds the believers that he and Silas and Timothy worked night and day, (presumably in tentmaking, as that had been part of Paul's training as a Pharisee before encountering the risen Lord Jesus on the Damascus road), that they might not be a burden to the church while they preached the gospel of God. (1 Thessalonians 2:9).

The gospel was the free grace of God to them. How then could the apostles rely on financial or material help or make themselves burdensome to these believers? How could there even be a suggestion that they preached the gospel for money, or for any material prosperity the gospel could bring them?

This was not ostentation but loving care for the believers who 'were witnesses, and God also, how holy and righteous and blameless' was their behaviour. (1 Thessalonians 2:10). Paul and Silas and Timothy, but perhaps especially Paul, were trying to impress upon the Thessalonians the principles on which they proclaimed the good news of Jesus.

This was only twenty years after His death, resurrection and ascension to the Father. To proclaim the gospel was a very precious gift from God, that they, as the servants of the Lord, should be entrusted with leading men and women to the place where they could enter into a relationship with God through our Lord Jesus Christ, could receive forgiveness of their sins and new life in Him.

But it was a very new experience and certain principles were being explored by the apostles for the future, and always under the first principle that 'Jesus is Lord'. (1 Corinthians 12:1), followed by the recognition that this declaration can only be validated in the life of the believer by the Holy Spirit.

This is closely followed by their overriding motivation, that everything that the apostles said and did was in love. As the apostles projected love towards these believers, so the believers projected love towards one another and to those around them.. This was totally consonant with what the Lord Jesus had said to His disciples at their last supper together. He said, 'A new commandment I give to you that you love one another as I have loved you. By this shall all men know that you are My disciples if you have love one for another'. (John 13:34).

This is the standard. This is the test to which Paul refers in 1 Thessalonians 2:4. This is what brings pleasure to the heart of God. This is the whole purpose of their being in Thessalonica at all, and the reason why God could entrust them with the gospel. It was a huge responsibility but also the sublimest privilege; and the reward was being approved by God, winning His approval, (1 Thessalonians 2:4). Paul had earlier described it as 'faith working through love'. (Galatians 5:6).

Further evidence of this love of Paul for the Thessalonians is shown by his describing himself as a father to them. He says, you know how, like a father with his children, we exhorted each one of you and encouraged you and charged you to lead a life worthy of God who calls you into His kingdom and glory. (1 Thessalonians 2:11).

Paul does not assume that all fathers are like this with their children, but he uses the words, 'you know, you remember, you are witnesses'. (1 Thessalonians 2:1,2,5,11; 2:9,10), to emphasise that this was indeed his attitude towards them. He had been with them like a comforting mother. (1 Thessalonians 2:7). Now he was instructing them like a wise father, for they could not remain as children, but had to grow up in the faith, to come to maturity, that they might come to 'the unity of the faith, and of the knowledge of the Son of God to mature manhood, to the measure of the stature of the fullness of Christ', (Ephesians 4:15), and 'speaking the truth in love might grow up in all things into Him who is the Head, even Christ'. (Ephesian 4:15).

Encouraging them, comforting them, exhorting them, and charging them to live a life worthy of God, Paul is able, yet again, as he had at the very beginning of his letter, to give thanks to God for them, constantly, (1 Thessalonians 2:3), seeing his beloved children receive the word of God as it truly is, not adulterated with lack of integrity or financial demands or the word of men; but the word of God, a word which brings to light the hidden things of darkness and sets men and women free. (1 Corinthians 4:5).

The word is an accomplishing and redeeming and creative word 'at work in all you who believe; (1 Thessalonians 2:13), with all the nature and character and power of God behind it. And though, like a wise father, Paul sometimes speaks to all his children together, he acknowledges each one individually, knowing that each one was called personally into God's kingdom and glory. (1 Thessalonians 2:11).

Paul is setting a really high standard for evangelists. A really committed evangelist could even echo the words of the psalmist. Such knowledge is too wonderful for me. It is high. How can I attain it ?' (Psalm 139:6). And many evangelists devoted to the preaching of the gospel may well feel the same. All that can be said is that Paul was not relying on his own ability; nor even on his own inability, for he confessed to the Corinthians that his word to them came in weakness, and fear, and much trembling, (1 Corinthians 2:3), but also in demonstration of the Spirit and the power of God. (1 Corinthians 2:4).

Paul was trembling before them, but he determined to know nothing among them but Jesus Christ and Him crucified. And God honoured his preaching, the preaching of the cross. For some it may be a help to do a course in public speaking but Paul did not have that. But he had the witness of the Holy Spirit, and God will always honour that which glorifies His Son. And Paul thanked God that what the Thessalonians received was the word of God, and they accepted it, not as the word of men, but as what it truly was, the word of God, at work in them as those who had become followers of the Lord Jesus. (1 Thessalonians 2:13).

1 Thessalonians 2:13-20. The results of evangelism.

We also thank God constantly for this, that when you received the word of God which you heard from us, you accepted it, not as the word of men, but as what it truly is, the word of God which is at work in you believers. For you brethren, became imitators of the churches of God in Christ Jesus which are in Judea, for you suffered the same things from your own countrymen as they did from the Jews,who killed both the Lord Jesus and the prophets and drove us out. (1 Thessalonians 2:13-15).

Though of course the result of the preaching of the gospel, the word of God, to the Thessalonians, goes far beyond the pages of these two letters written by Paul, yet as he is writing to the Thessalonians he notices two things.

First, that they have become imitators of the churches of God in Christ Jesus which are in Judea. (1 Thessalonians 2:14).

This did not mean that they were slavishly following rules and regulations set out by the church in Jerusalem, the most prominent of the churches in Judea, but that they had discovered as had those who had come to faith in Jerusalem on the Day of Pentecost, that they wanted to sit at the feet of the apostles, and listen to their teaching; they wanted to share meals together in which they probably remembered the Lord Jesus in the breaking of bread; they felt the need of fellowship together and prayer together. (Acts 2:42).

They had suddenly discovered themselves to be a family, brothers and sisters in Christ. They were discovering a different way of living, of compassion and forgiveness towards one another; of forbearance of each other; of the peace of God ruling their hearts; of allowing His word to dwell in them richly; even singing together in psalms and hymns and spiritual songs, singing and making melody in their hearts to the Lord, in worship to Him who had done so much for them. (Colossians 3:12-16).

This may present a cosy picture of life after receiving the word of God. But together with all the positive and life affirming experiences that were happening to them, they were learning, *secondly*, how to suffer, like the churches in Judea. (1 Thessalonians 2:14).

The churches in Judea had suffered many things from their own countrymen and now the Thessalonian believers were doing the same. The Jews had killed both the Lord Jesus and the prophets and the apostles were in the same direct line. They had been driven out by those men who were not only displeasing God, and opposing His word, but were also hindering the apostles from speaking to the Gentiles that they might be saved. And it was not only the apostles who suffered but the whole church. (Acts 8;1; 1 Thessalonians 2: 14-16).

In this way, the church at Thessalonica was imitating the churches of Judea, (Acts 8:1), finding themselves facing the same kind of opposition, suffering the same kind of persecution.

This was the second thing that Paul had noticed as a result of evangelism, that there was a price to pay for receiving the word of God. Jesus had forewarned them. He had said to His disciples, 'In the world you will have tribulation, but be of good cheer, I have overcome the world'. (John 16:33). And He had also previously said, 'in Me you may have peace'. (John 16:33). The peace of the Lord Jesus, the knowledge that He has overcome the world does not negate the suffering, but it gives the suffering purpose.

On another occasion, when Paul wanted to strengthen the souls of the disciples in the Ephesian church, he said to their elders that it is through much tribulation that we must enter the kingdom of God. (Acts 20:22). Do we want to reign with Him, to see a kingdom in which all that opposes Him will have been done away with, when He takes His power and reigns? Do we want to see that glorious time when the King is revealed in all His beauty and we are permitted to sit with Him in His kingdom?

The Thessalonian believers were certainly learning that through much tribulation. they would be part of that kingdom. They were learning to trust Him more. Would they have preferred not to have been troubled by these apostles, whom the Jews described as those who had turned the world upside down? (Acts 17:6). Or would they have preferred to stay with what those Jews would have described as the right way up? It was true that these men of God had brought a disturbing message with them to Thessalonica.

Paul is concerned for them. He is writing to them from Corinth, to his beloved children in the faith and he is longing to see them, and so grateful to Timothy who was in Corinth with him, for bringing back a report from Thessalonica, assuring him that the believers are 'standing fast in the Lord'. (1 Thessalonians 3:8). They have suffered, and it may well be that they are still suffering, but their suffering has made them stronger, more determined than ever to stand fast in the Lord, to stand firm in the faith, especially as others seeing their steadfastness in the face of persecution have also turned to the Lord.

Their faith, their trust in the Risen Lord Jesus and His great love for them is worth suffering for, if it brings glory to Him.

Many today are suffering for their faith, and even for those not undergoing persecution, suffering is part of human existence, part of the fabric of life. But the word remains true. 'In all their afflictions He was afflicted, and the angel of His presence saved them. In HIs love and in His pity He redeemed them. He lifted them up and carried them all the days of old'. (Isaiah 63:9).

To be lifted up and be carried by the Lord Jesus is consolation enough. In times of trouble, we may not always be aware of the everlasting arms underneath us, (Deuteronomy 33:27), but when we look back, we see and understand that without His strong arms about us we would not have survived. This is the steadfast love of the Lord towards us. He is glorious in His faithfulness. His mercies never come to an end. (Lamentations 3:22).

Paul, who went through much tribulation, is able to confirm that 'this light affliction which is but for a moment, is preparing for us an eternal weight of glory beyond all comparison'. (2 Corinthians 4:17). To live in the good of that is to hold everything in perspective.

The Thessalonian believers were already 'heirs of the kingdom of God and His glory' (1 Thessalonians 2:12). And they have the comfort of knowing that they are not alone. As the churches of God in Judea, including Jerusalem, have suffered for their faith, so they too, the churches of Macedonia, and particularly that of Thessalonica are suffering. In this they are one with the Judean churches, 'imitators' of them. They all belong to the same Lord, they have all received the word of the Lord in penitence and faith and they are all living under the guidance of the indwelling Holy Spirit. They are fellow members of the Body of Christ. They are part of the fellowship, the love which binds all together in perfect harmony, (Colossians 3:14), all sustained by the life of the Lord Jesus, their risen and ascended Lord.

The Thessalonians had received the word of the Lord 'in much affliction' but also 'with joy inspired by the Holy Spirit', (1 Thessalonians 1:6). This joy may be said to account for the genuineness of the faith of those who suffer for it. (Bruce p 50). They could have renounced their faith under those conditions, but that would have been to lose their newfound joy, their fellowship with other believers, their new life as they enjoyed the love of their new family and the knowledge day by day of the great love and grace being showered upon them by God, in Christ.

Paul, writing six years later to the Corinthian church, is still commending the churches of Macedonia; that through the grace of God, though being severely tested and in a situation of severe poverty, they are still giving beyond their means to the support of those among the poor of Jerusalem. (2 Corinthians 8:1-4). And he repeats this in his letter to the Romans. (Romans 15:25,26).

There is more than a suggestion here that all the churches in Macedonia are in fellowship with each other, including the church of Thessalonica. Could the severe testing of which Paul writes have brought them together? And their extreme poverty the result of continuing persecution? Paul can only say, 'You know the grace of our Lord Jesus Christ, that though He was rich, yet for our sakes He became poor, that we through His poverty might become rich'. (2 Corinthians 8:9).

The Thessalonian church and all the churches of Macedonia have been enriched , not with earthly riches, but by riches beyond price, through the grace of our Lord Jesus Christ. And their disbursement of what earthly riches they may possess overflows in thanksgiving to God and glory to Him; not only by supplying the wants of their brothers and sisters, but by assuring them of their love and concern for them. It is what is meant by being part of the Body of Christ.

1 Thessalonians 2:17. Plans for a second visit to Thessalonica.

But since we were bereft of you brethren, for a short time, in person if not in heart, we endeavoured the more eagerly and with great desire to see you face to face, because we wanted to come to you; I, Paul, again and again; but Satan hindered us. (1 Thessalonians 2:17-18).

Satan, the adversary of God, has only limited power, but he is active in putting obstacles in the way of the children of God. (Bruce p 55). Paul was not using a figurative expression. There is a reality behind the words he uses. But like the thorn in the flesh, 'the messenger of Satan to buffet him', (2 Corinthians 12:7), Satan's activity is nullified, made of no effect by the purpose of God in allowing it. Paul realises that the thorn in the flesh allows God's grace to be sufficient for Paul, for HIs power is made perfect in Paul's weakness. So he says, 'I will all the more gladly boast of my weakness that the power of Christ may *rest* upon me, may *cover* me like a tent'. To know the covering of the Lord Jesus upon him more than compensated for any buffeting of Satan which he may have endured.

But not to be able to visit his beloved Thessalonians was a real problem for Paul. It must be very seldom that being unable to see one's friends, even for a short time, is equivalent to a state of bereavement. But this was what Paul felt about the lack of seeing his 'brethren', his brothers and sisters in Christ, face to face. (1 Thessalonians 2:17). God had wrought within him such a depth of love for these men and women. He felt towards them as a gentle mother, (1 Thessalonians 2:7), or a wise father, (1 Thessalonians 2:11). They were his hope, his joy and crown of boasting before the Lord Jesus at His coming, They were his glory and his joy. (1 Thessalonians 2:19). (Bruce p 56).

Paul and Silas and Timothy had been faithful stewards of the mysteries of God, and it is required of stewards that they are found trustworthy. (1 Corinthians 4:1,2). But the Thessalonians had become so much more to them than recipients of the gospel, the mysteries of God.

1 Thessalonians Chapter 3

1 Thessalonians 3:1-13. Timothy returns from Thessalonica.

Therefore, says Paul, when we could bear it no longer, we were willing to be left behind at Athens alone, and we sent Timothy, our brother and God's servant in the gospel of Christ, to establish you in your faith and to exhort you that no one be moved by these afflictions. For when we were with you, we told you beforehand that we were to suffer affliction; just as it has come to pass, and as you know. For this reason, when I could bear it no longer, I sent that I might know your faith, for fear that the tempter had tempted you and that our labour would be in vain. (1 Thessalonians 3:1-5).

Paul says, 'when we could bear it no longer', not knowing how these beloved believers had survived the latest time of opposition. Though Paul had been sent to Athens, and was waiting for Silas and Timothy to join him, he was willing to be left behind in Athens alone so that Timothy could go back to Thessalonica and see for himself their faith and how they were responding in this time of affliction. (1 Thessalonians 3: 1-4). Paul repeats,'when I could bear it no longer, I sent that I might know your faith, for fear that somehow the tempter had tempted you and that our labour would be in vain. (1 Thessalonians 3:5). Paul is full of apprehension in case the tempter, the spiritual enemy of God and of His people should succeed in damaging their faith, of denying them all the blessings they had derived from Paul's ministry among them, emptying his preaching of all its life giving meaning.

How grateful he was when Timothy reported back the 'good news of their faith and love', and their kindly remembrance of

Paul, longing to see him and Silas, just as Paul and Silas longed to see them. (1 Thessalonians 3:6).

This was so comforting to Paul. Though he was now in Corinth, (Acts 18:1), and the situation in Corinth was causing him difficulties, indeed causing him distress, (1 Thessalonians 3:7), he was comforted by the continuing faith of the Thessalonian believers, and once again in this letter, is full of thanksgiving to God for all the joy these brothers and sisters have brought him. The happy report from Timothy does not prevent him from praying earnestly night and day, that he might see them face to face and supply what is lacking in their faith. (1 Thessalonians 3:6-11).

He prayed that 'our God and Father Himself and our Lord Jesus Christ may direct our way to you', and that the Lord might make them to increase and abound in love to one another and to all men, and that He might 'establish their hearts unblameable in holiness before our God and Father, at the coming of the Lord Jesus with all the saints'. (1 Thessalonians 3:11-13).

This was quite a prayer. This is 50 A.D. Paul did not know whether he would ever be able to go back to Macedonia, and particularly Thessalonica, though there is evidence to suggest that he may have done, especially in 2 Corinthians 2:13; 7:5; and 9:2, even though it may have been a brief visit as he travelled through Macedonia to Judea with the collection for the believers in Jerusalem in 55 A.D. (2 Corinthians 1:16).

The Thessalonian believers were Paul's 'crown of boasting', his glory and his joy, (1 Thessalonians 2:19), as he saw the grace of God at work in them; another example of the transforming power of the Holy Spirit. But that did not mean that he could neglect to pray for them. Timothy's visit to the Thessalonians encouraged both them and Paul, as Timothy reported back to him the faithfulness of the Thessalonians.

Paul's time with them had not been extensive, and all too soon he had then been escorted to Beroea from Thessalonica after the crowd had been incited to riot. (Acts 17:5). From Beroea, Paul had gone to Athens after another projected riot in Beroea by the Thessalonian Jews, where he waited somewhat impatiently for news of the Thessalonian believers. Were they alright? What had happened in Beroea after he had left? When could he expect Silas and Timothy to join him? (Acts 17:15).

Of course, while Paul was waiting in Athens, he did not neglect the opportunity to engage the Athenians in debate over the plurality of the objects of their worship. (Acts 17:23), but having sent a message to Silas and Timothy, he was longing for their arrival. They did indeed intend to follow Paul to Athens, but by this time he had moved on to Corinth, and they discovered Paul staying with Priscilla and Aquila, who like him were tentmakers. (Acts 18:1,2,5).

When Silas and Timothy arrived in Corinth from Macedonia, Paul was occupied with preaching, testifying to the Jews in Corinth that the Christ was Jesus. (Acts 18:5). But Paul, concerned for the Thessalonians, sent Timothy, with the consent of Silas, back to Thessalonica, to encourage them and establish them in the faith. (1 Thessalonians 3:2).

Timothy was highly esteemed by Paul. He calls him 'our brother and God's servant in the gospel of Christ'. (1 Thessalonians 3:2). Paul uses the plural, 'our brother', indicating that it was he and Silas together who valued Timothy's ministry, and who took the decision to suggest that Timothy return to Thessalonica to establish the Thessalonians in their faith and to exhort them that none of them should be moved by the affliction they were suffering. (1 Thessalonians 3:2).

Faithful Timothy, whom Paul describes in 1 Corinthians 4:17 as 'my beloved and faithful child in the Lord', and in Philippians 2:22, that 'as a son with his father he served with me in the gospel', returned to Paul in Corinth with the information which he so longed for, that the young church, though suffering affliction were strong in faith and love, (1 Thessalonians 3:6), and there was no need for these believers who were still young in the faith, to be disturbed or perturbed, for Paul had told them beforehand that they would suffer affliction, just as it had come to pass. (1 Thessalonians 3:4).

So now Paul, having travelled from Athens to Corinth, was actively engaged in preaching to the Corinthians, testifying once again to the Jews that the Christ was Jesus. (Acts 18:5). But he was still concerned about what was happening in Thessalonica, eagerly, intensely, longing to see his beloved children in the faith. Paul had now travelled from Macedonia, in northern Greece, to Corinth in Achaia, southern Greece, and the report from Timothy encouraged him to believe that what the Holy Spirit had accomplished in Macedonia, He was also able to accomplish in Achaia. This was an important encouragement to Paul as he faced many difficulties in the Corinthian church. He was greatly distressed by the Corinthian believers and while he gave thanks to God for them, (1 Corinthians 1:4,10), he was overjoyed at the evidence of lives which were being lived which were worthy of the gospel, in Thessalonica. He says, 'we live, if you stand fast in the Lord'. (1 Thessalonians 3:8).

He is full of thanksgiving to God for them, full of joy for answered prayer which he and Silas had offered night and day and continued to offer, earnestly praying that they might have the joy of seeing them face to face and supplying what was lacking in their faith. 'May our God and Father Himself, and our Lord Jesus direct our way to you', Paul prays. And it appears that five years later, that prayer was answered. (1 Thessalonians 3:11,13). And he and Silas pray that the Lord will establish the hearts of the Thessalonians 'unblameable in holiness before our God and Father, at the coming of the Lord Jesus with all His saints'. And that that prayer too will be answered. (1 Thessalonians 3:13).

This is the day that is coming, the day of the coming of the Lord Jesus with all His saints. This fact, the future coming of our Lord Jesus in power and great glory, gives to the Thessalonian Christians the incentive for holy living, to live to please God, to be the saints, the sanctified ones, the believing men and women whom the Lord will bring with Him when He comes. (2 Thessalonians 1:10).

So Paul proceeds to explain to the Thessalonians how sanctification takes place both physically and materially in the context of spirituality.

1 Thessalonians Chapter 4

1 Thessalonians 4:1-12. Practical aspects of sanctification.

Finally, brethren, we beseech and exhort you in the Lord Jesus, that as you learned from us how you ought to live and to please God, just as you are doing, you do so more and more. For you know what instructions we gave you through the Lord Jesus. For this is the will of God, even your sanctification, that you abstain from unchastity; that each one knows how to take a wife for himself in holiness and honour. (1 Thessalonians 4:1-4).

Paul writes, 'Finally brethren', indicating that he has a last but very important thing to say to them. He writes,'This is the will of God, even your sanctification'. He is not saying that God wants them to be pious or legalistic, but sanctified, made holy, set apart for God. And he defines sanctification in this way. He says, 'You learned from us how you ought to live and to please God; just as you are doing, you do so more and more. For you know what instructions we gave you through the Lord Jesus. (1 Thessalonians 4:1).

Does this appear to be too simplistic? Or prescriptive? Ought carries the connotation of 'must'. That as they had learned from Paul and Silas how they ought to live and to please God, this is what they must do and do it more and more? But these were apparently the instructions Paul and Silas gave them through the Lord Jesus, so they carried dominical weight. (1 Thessalonians 4:2).

Sanctification promises so much. It is to be holy before the Lord for He says, 'Be holy for I am holy'. (Leviticus 11:44,45). Or in

Peter's rendering of the words as a promise, 'You *shall* be holy for I am holy', (1 Peter 1:16), for *this is the intention and purpose and promise of God.* This is the will of God, says Paul, this is what He wants for you, even your sanctification. And yet the promise apparently delivers so little if all that it entails is following the instructions of the apostles, even if given through the Lord Jesus, for sanctification is not an improving set of rules or an exalted standard of moral behaviour but the setting apart of a life to God, separated from all that would hinder communion with Him, everything that would deny that separation *unto Him,* and separation *from the world.*

Sanctification, then, is not just another set of rules, a particularly high standard of ethical behaviour. As Paul writes to the Thessalonian believers, it appears that sanctification is the practical result of while being alive to God, they should also be concerned with the relationship between husbands and wives, with abstaining from unchastity, from adultery, from fornication; and above all, with their attitude towards one another. It is living quietly and unostentatiously before their neighbours, making provision for their families so that they may 'command the respect of outsiders and be dependent on nobody'. (1 Thessalonians 3:3-11).

This is what is meant by living a sanctified life according to Paul. It appears to be a mundane, not very exciting experience as Paul describes it. Can the attitude of a believer towards his wife, or being dependent on nobody, but working hard to supply the needs of his family be evidence of a sanctified life? We can perhaps see some work of sanctification in the lives of those previously driven by unchastity, but who now needed to take a wife for themselves in holiness and honour, (1 Thessalonians 4:3), and to learn how not to transgress his brother in the matter. (1 Thessalonians 4:6), for God has not called us to impurity, but sanctification. And there is no doubt that learning from Paul and Silas how to live and please God is valuable, a good thing and memorable, for this is the will of God for the believers.

But from Paul's perspective, this is the great truth of sanctification, to live a life well pleasing to God for He has so much in view for them, and the practical aspects of life really matter. As Paul wrote to the believers in Philippi,' He who began a good work in you will perform it to the day of Jesus Christ'. (Philippians 1:6). *Sanctification is the work of the Holy Spirit in the life of the believer* and at the end of this first letter to the Thessalonians, Paul writes, 'May the God of peace Himself sanctify you wholly, and may your spirit, soul and body be kept sound and blameless at the coming of our Lord Jesus Christ'. (1 Thessalonians 5:25,26). *He who has called you is faithful, and He will do it. (1 Thessalonians 5:25.26).*

Sanctification is not just another set of rules, perhaps a higher law than the law previously attempted by devout Jews. Sanctification is also a completely different concept from keeping the law, it is a new way of living, a different approach to all the practical demands of life; as indeed is the truth of justification.

Justification, as we have seen, is being made righteous. We are justified, made righteous by faith, and this not of ourselves, it is the gift of God, not of works lest anyone should boast. (Romans 5:2; Ephesians 2:8,9). This gift of faith enables the free gift of righteousness to be given to those who receive the abundance of His grace. (Romans 5:17). The free gift of faith is followed by the free gift of righteousness, freely given because we can contribute nothing. There is nothing in us which explains such munificence on the part of God. God shows His forgiving love for us in that while we were yet sinners, Christ died for us, and we are justified by His blood. (Romans 5:8).

Because we were sinners we were condemned to the judgement of the wrath of God, not as though God was subject to irrational passions like uncontrollable anger, or wrath, for that would be to anthropomorphize God, but His wrath as His constant beneficent pressure against all evil and ungodliness, and wickedness of men, who by their wickedness suppress the truth. (Romans 1:18).The wrath of God is His justice, His condemnation against evil, His righteous judgement on those who do not obey the truth. (Romans 2:8).The absolute moral perfection of God demands that what is disobedience to Him must be challenged and destroyed, for there cannot be two inherently contrary and contradictory systems of thought, each claiming to be the truth by which men and women live.

But Jesus found a way to enable men and women to live in the righteousness of God. He took all the wrath of God that was justly against us because of our sin, our disobedience, and cancelled the bond of the sentence of death which was against us, nailing it to His cross. (Colossians 2:14). Instead of His wrath, His judgement, resting on us, the wrath of God, His judgement, rested on His beloved Son as He hung upon the cross, and Jesus bore that wrath, crying out in His agony, 'My God, My God, why have you forsaken Me?' (Matthew 27:46; Mark 15:34). Jesus took that sin down into death and left it there when He rose from the dead. He died for us. He was wounded for our transgressions. He was bruised for our iniquities. The chastisement of our peace was upon Him, and with His stripes we are healed. (Isaiah 53:5).

He took that judgement upon Himself that we might go free. He did it for us that we might be reconciled to God by the death of His Son. (Romans 5:10). This is His gift to us, the gift of justification, of righteousness, His righteousness, and freedom from sin as we receive eternal life through Jesus Christ our Lord. (Romans 5:8). This is our justification, the *immediate response of God in response to faith in His beloved Son.*

But sanctification is a *process*, and is the work of the Holy Spirit. Since we are now justified by faith, we may present our bodies to be a living sacrifice, holy and acceptable to God, which is our spiritual worship. And Paul continues, be not *conformed* to this world, but be *transformed* by the renewing of your mind. (Romans 12:1,2). Our minds need to be renewed for we need to understand as we appropriate spiritual truths, and especially to understand what is the good and perfect and acceptable will of God. (Romans 12:2).

If we are *conformed* to the world, there is a dissonance, a dissociation between our outward living and the inner reality. If we are *transformed*, our outward living becomes the outward expression of the inner reality. So we need the work of the Holy Spirit. God wants us to be transformed, by the Holy Spirit, for He wants us to enjoy the blessings of the kingdom of God.

For the kingdom of God is not food or drink or any other appetites which we may or may not have, but *righteousness and peace and joy in the Holy Spirit. (Romans 14:17). And He is the reality within us as we seek not to quench Him, (Ephesians 4:30), or to grieve Him, (1 Thessalonians 5:19), but to yield to His work in us.* For we are predestined to be conformed, not to the world, but to the image of His Son, that He might be the firstborn among many brethren. (Romans 8:29). We are destined and appointed to live to the praise of His glory, who first trusted in Christ. (Ephesians 1:12). This is sanctification.

Paul gives the Thessalonian believers a hint as to how to live the Spirit filled, sanctified, life. First, he says that he is praying earnestly for them, and how important it is that we should pray for one another. (1 Thessalonians 3:10). And then that what he is praying for them is that the Lord will make them increase and abound in love more and more, to one another and to all men, so that the Lord may establish their hearts 'unblameable before our God and Father at the coming of our Lord Jesus with all His saints'. (1 Thessalonians 3:11-13). It is the principle of Galatians 5:6; faith working through love, for love is the principle of sanctification.

This is the way of holiness, the self renouncing, self giving love that reflects the love of Jesus and glorifies Him, His extravagant, self denying love.

Paul has probably quite unselfconsciously demonstrated his love for the Thessalonians in this letter. He says, 'you know what instructions we gave you'. (1 Thessalonians 4:2), and no doubt these instructions were very helpful and useful to them as they sat at his feet and absorbed all that he had to tell them of the mysteries of God. But even more inspiring was his life lived among them; his 'motherhood' of them, so gentle; his 'fatherhood' of them, so wise; his labour among them night and day that he might not be a burden to them; and now his encouraging letter to them, full of thankfulness to God for them. (1 Thessalonians 2: 7-11).

Throughout this letter, Paul could not have more consistently insisted on his love for them, expressing his love for them and encouraging their love for one another. To the Ephesians he writes that speaking the truth, the wonderful truth of the gospel, in love, is the way to spiritual maturity. 'Speaking the truth in love, we are able to grow up in every way into Him who is the Head, even Christ'. (Ephesians 4:15).

Saved by grace, justified by grace, sanctified by grace, all is of Jesus whom God has made our wisdom, our righteousness, our sanctification, and our redemption. Therefore it is written, 'Let him who boasts, let him boast of the Lord. (1 Corinthians 1:30). And it seems that sanctification can be summed up in one word, *love*. Love for our Father in heaven, for the Lord Jesus Christ and for the Holy Spirit; and love in all our dealings with our families, with others, and especially with those who are of the household of faith. (Galatians 6:10).

Under the old covenant, the priests were sanctified, set apart for the work of the tabernacle to which God had called them. So as believers, men and women may be set apart to God, not necessarily in an official ecclesiastical way, as were the priests, but in their sometimes apparently humdrum lives, living apart unto Him, receiving from Him such an abundance of love, that

that love overflows to Him and to others, and whose only concern is that all the glory goes to Him.

Paul is convinced that this is the case already with the Thessalonians, for writing a letter, five years later, to the Corinthian believers, he notes in 2 Corinthians 8:1, that they, along with all the churches of Macedonia, including Thessalonica, are inspired by the grace of God, even though they are living in a time of affliction. They are inspired to send relief to the churches in Judea and the church in Jerusalem. (2 Corinthians 8:1; Romans 16:26). Paul had noted five years earlier in writing to the Thessalonians that concerning love of the brethren, their brothers and sisters in Christ, they had no need that anyone should write to them, for they themselves had been taught of God to love one another; and indeed they did love all the brethren in Macedonia, and did so more and more. (1 Thessalonians 4:1,9,10).

Does this mean that moral instruction is unnecessary? As some believers, newly liberated from the constraints of the law, will have said to Paul, and are quoted by him in Romans 6:14, as saying, 'we are no longer under law, we no longer need to obey the law, for we are under grace'. This of course is true. Men and women who have come to Christ no longer need to submit to the Mosaic law, to the ten commandments or to man made rules and regulations, for Christ has set them free. Can they not therefore do as they like because they are not under the law but under grace?

Paul agrees. How can anyone who has died to sin and been united through baptism with Christ in a resurrection like His, (Romans 6:5) be anything but free, free from sin, free from the necessity of obeying the law to which we were all once slaves? They are free from condemnation. (Romans 8:1). But the very fact of being dead to sin makes us alive to God in Christ Jesus. (Romans 6:11). And this fact, of being alive to Him, is the very reason why we yield to Him as people who have been brought from death to life. Now we have been set free from slavery to sin. We are no longer slaves to sin. We have become slaves to God, and we may receive the free gift of sanctification and its outcome, eternal life. (Romans 6:22).

Believers serve God, not in the old written code but in the new life of the Spirit. (Romans 7:6). They turn to Christ in faith for deliverance from the law and are given a new law, 'the law of the Spirit of life in Christ Jesus which sets them free from the law of sin and death. (Romans 8:1). The Spirit Himself has come to them, setting them free! They are living under the Spirit's control, the law of the Spirit of life. But this does not give them the right to sin *but the ability not to sin,* to be obedient to righteousness, yielding their members to righteousness for sanctification. (Romans 6:23).

But *if they sin,* they have an advocate with the Father, Jesus Christ the righteous, and He is the propitiation, the atoning sacrifice for their sin. (1 John 2:1).

This is already happening for the Thessalonian believers. Paul's primary instruction is that they should not quench the Spirit. (1 Thessalonians 5:19). The word *'quench'* is a serious word. It is like blowing out a candle. It can mean to extinguish the activity of the Holy Spirit, for it is through His activity in their hearts that they become obedient to righteousness. If we begin by quenching the Spirit, we may lose our discernment, our ability to test everything by the Spirit. We may neglect to hold fast that which is good and to abstain from every form of evil. (1 Thessalonians 5:19-22). Paul prays for them, that God Himself may sanctify them wholly in spirit, soul and body, and he declares his utter conviction that God will answer his prayer. God is faithful, and He will do it. (1 Thessalonians 5:25). Justification is immediate. Sanctification takes a little more time. But God is faithful.

So we begin to appreciate that sanctification is not an increase in acceptably moral behaviour, but a constant and continuing reliance on the Holy Spirit, the One whose whole purpose is to glorify Jesus and who will glorify Him in and through us. (John 16:14). Jesus said, 'The Holy Spirit will take what is mine and will declare it to you. And He will guide you into all truth. (John 14:13).

There is always room for growth, as Paul says, 'we exhort you brethren to love one another, and to do so more and more'. (1 Thessalonians 4:10).. As men and women come to Christ, the process begins, and by God's grace and the faithfulness of the Holy Spirit, continues, until they all attain to the unity of the faith, and the knowledge of the Son of God to mature manhood, to the measure of the stature of the fulness of Christ, and speaking the truth in love my grow up in every way into Him, who is the Head, into Christ. (Ephesians 4:3-15).

Paul's 'instruction' is not a basic attempt to engage the Thessalonians in a life of morality, but an encouragement to them to walk in the Spirit, to be aware of the still, small voice of His presence, of His leading and comforting and counselling and encouragement. This is so much more life affirming than a series of do's and don'ts, but it requires a sensitivity to Him and to the word of God through Him. We are thankful that the Lord Jesus sent the Holy Spirit in His Name to teach us all things and to bring to our remembrance all that He said while He was on earth, (John 14:26), and to God who gave His Holy Spirit to us. (1 Thessalonians 4:8).

Our aim is not to lead ethically or morally circumspect lives, but to live as those who have been redeemed from the curse of the law and are now living 'by faith in the Son of God who loved me and gave Himself for me'. (Galatians 3:13,21; 2:20).

There is a sense in which believers are already sanctified, chosen by God who sees the end from the beginning, (1 Thessalonians

1:4), separated from the world, set apart for God, for this is what being a saint, being sanctified, means. But God never forces His will on any one, and Peter sees the need to encourage the readers of his second letter to make their calling and election sure, (2 Peter 1:10), to live in the good of this election, this choosing of them by God, this separation from anything in the world which would hinder their relationship with Him through the Holy Spirit. To make actual what is potential.

Although the Corinthian Christians were troubled by some among them who were leading immoral lives. Paul reminded them that 'such were some of you, but you are washed, you are sanctified, you are justified in the Name of the Lord Jesus Christ and in the Spirit of our God'. He continues, 'Your body is a temple of the Holy Spirit within you, which you have from God. You are not your own, you are bought with a price. So glorify God in your body. (1 Corinthians 6:11, 19).

And again, 'you are bought with a price; do not become slaves of men'. (1 Corinthians 7:23). We come to Christ with all our sin, and we are washed, cleansed from our sin through the atoning sacrifice of Christ. And we are set apart. Day by day, as we trust in Him, we are being conformed to the image of His Son. (Romans 8:29). This is sanctification, and it leads to the final state which God predetermined, predestined, preordained, that we should arrive at the state of holiness; for He has said, 'You *shall* be holy, for I am holy'. God always fulfils all His promises.

This is His promise to us. He wants us to see Him, and without holiness, no one can see the Lord. (Hebrews 12:14). Now we may see in a glass darkly, in a mirror dimly, (1 Corinthians 13:12), but then we shall see Him face to face. This is the Christian hope, to see Jesus. And when we see Him we shall be like Him for we shall see Him as He is. And everyone who has this hope purifies himself even as He is pure (1 John 3:3).

Paul speaks of the cost of redemption. You were bought with a price, he says; recognizing the eternal significance of the blood shed by Christ on the cross. Jesus shed His blood in redeeming power, to take away the sin of the world. It was redeeming in intention and execution, fully and freely available to all, but at tremendous cost to Him. This is the cost of which Paul speaks. 'You were bought with a price, therefore glorify God in your body and in your spirit which are God's'. (1 Corinthians 6:20).

With what joy then do believers present their bodies as a living sacrifice to God, holy and acceptable to Him, which is our spiritual worship. (Romans 12:1). How could they do otherwise? There is nothing in them which could possibly compensate for His great love for them. All the recompense they could possibly make is to love Him in return, to yield their lives to Him in humble submission, in obedience to all that the Holy Spirit shows them; in a daily offering of worship to Him, for He is our God. The Lord loves us as we are. But He does not want us to stay as we are. (a quotation from Rev.David Harris).

If the life of John the Baptist had no other purpose, the significance of His ministry lay in this, that he was given the revelation that Jesus was the Lamb of God who takes away the sin of the world, a revelation of paramount spiritual importance., for He had the whole world in His purview. (John 1:29). And He takes away our sin, setting us free from the law of sin and death. (Romans 8:2), giving us a new law, the law of the Spirit of life in Christ Jesus.

1 Thessalonians 4:13-18. Problems with the Parousia, the second coming of Christ.

But we would not have you ignorant, brethren, concerning those who are asleep, that you may not grieve as others do who have no hope. For since we believe that Jesus died and rose again, even so through Jesus, God will bring with Him those who have fallen asleep. For this we declare to you by the word of the Lord, that we who are alive, who are left until the coming of the Lord, shall not precede those who have fallen asleep. For the Lord himself will descend from heaven with a cry of command, with the archangel's call and with the sound of the trumpet of God. (1 Thessalonians 4:13-16).

The Greek word, *parousia,* means arrival, coming, or presence and in Greek literature was frequently employed with reference to a special visitation by a ruler or god. Translated into English, it functions as a technical term for the coming of Christ at the end of human history.

Though the Thessalonian believers are commended by Paul for their determination to live and please God, and to do so more and more, (1 Thessalonians 4:2), they are not without confusion as to what will happen at the coming of the Lord Jesus with all His saints. (1 Thessalonians 3:3). This is important for us too. Although Paul had described the Thessalonians in this way as living as pleasing to God, they do not yet have perfect understanding. Sanctification does not signify perfection. There is always more to understand, more to appreciate of the purposes of God, more to learn about Jesus, more love for Him and more love for one another.

But what troubles Paul is the lack of understanding of these believers over a particular aspect of the *parousia.* Since becoming believers, they have entered into a loving relationship with others which they had not known before. And it seems that some of those whom they had loved had 'fallen asleep'. This is a euphemism used by Paul as a way of saying that they had died. (1 Thessalonians 4:13). This is causing them, not the normal grief of someone whom they love, dying, but the grief of not knowing what will become of them on the day when Jesus comes back to the earth to receive all His beloved sons and daughters to Himself; for they will not be here.

It appears that the Thessalonians already had some appreciation of the details concerning the coming again of the Lord Jesus, for they had turned from idols to serve the living and true God and to wait for His Son from heaven. (1 Thessalonians 1:9,10).

When Jesus had been taken up from His disciples into heaven on the occasion of His Ascension, two angel-men in white clothing had appeared to them, who told them quite clearly that this same Jesus, who had been taken from them into heaven, would come again in the same way that they had seen Him go into heaven. (Acts 1:10,11). And Jesus had faithfully revealed to His disciples as He sat with them on the mount of Olives, the signs of His coming and of the end of the age. (Matthew 24:1-51). Jesus had even told Caiaphas the High Priest when He was on trial before him that 'hereafter you will see the Son of Man seated at the right hand of power and coming on the clouds of heaven'. (Matthew 26:64).

The Thessalonians were not ignorant of the promise of His coming again. They were ignorant concerning those who had fallen asleep, and were grieving for them. (1 Thessalonians 4:13).

Paul does not imply that it is wrong to grieve. The death of those whom we love is very painful, and the more the love the more intense the pain. But Paul says, we do not grieve as those who have no hope. These believers knew that those who had fallen asleep in Jesus would awake to resurrection life.

Jesus had so clearly declared that He was the resurrection and the life. (John 11:25). No one who had come to Him and been identified with Him in His death and resurrection through the waters of baptism would remain in death. Those who had been baptized were baptized into His death, (Romans 6:4), but Jesus had said 'he who believes in Me , though he die, yet shall he live, and I will raise him up at the last day. Whoever lives and believes in Me shall never die'. (John 11:25,26). How could anyone, with the eternal life which the Lord Jesus gives to those who trust in Him, coursing within them as a result of their faith, believing on the Son of God, not be raised up to be with Him forever?

But the Thessalonians were not looking towards that time of tribulation, which was also the period of the beginning of sorrows, on the earth, which Jesus had assured them would surely come first, (Matthew 24:21), but for the day of His coming, His *parousia,* which will conclude with the day of judgement. (Matthew 24:30; 25;31). Then they will see the Son of Man coming on the clouds of heaven with power and great glory. And He will send forth His angels with a great trumpet and they will gather together His elect from the four winds, from one end of the heavens to the other. (Matthew 24:3).

How much of the teaching about the second coming of Christ had Paul and Silas been able to pass on to the Thessalonians in the short time they had had with them is debatable, as is also how much of the Lord's teaching while He was on earth had filtered through to the early church, for the Gospels were not written immediately after His death and resurrection.

But Paul has given the Thessalonians the confidence to believe that at the sound of the great trumpet of God, the Lord Himself will descend from Heaven with a shout, with the voice of the archangel; and the dead in Christ will rise first. Then we who are alive and remain will be caught up together, raptured together with them to meet the Lord in the air, and so shall we ever be with the Lord. (1 Thessalonians 4:16-18). Paul concludes, 'wherefore, comfort one another with these words'.

This could have been what Paul had learned from those privileged to have heard Jesus speak when He was on the earth, but what Paul also recognized was the ongoing phenomenon of the revelatory work of the Holy Spirit, which Paul values as a gift of the Holy Spirit to him, for he says, 'I will come to visions and revelations of the Lord'. (2 Corinthian 12:1).

As with all Paul's teaching, what he had been able to share with them, his beloved Thessalonians, about the *parousia,* the coming again of the Lord Jesus in power and great glory, they had received with open minds and hearts. How wonderful it would be to see Jesus coming in the clouds of heaven to receive from the earth all those who belonged to Him, for they believed that this great event could possibly happen within their lifetime. It is now about twenty years since the Lord had been taken from them into heaven. Perhaps He will come back soon?

Their concern had been about those who had fallen asleep, who were no longer here with them. But Paul says affectionately.' Brethren, do not sorrow like those who have no hope'. (1 Thessalonians 4:13). The tense of the verb points to a continuing sorrow. This is a very real grief to them. But it would be an even greater grief if they were without hope.

The Thessalonian believers were probably aware of the pagan beliefs of those around them, for they had formerly been pagans themselves. (1 Thessalonians 1:9,10). Nowhere, in all the literature of the time do we find any certainty of what happens after death; no hope of a life beyond the grave. There is no comfort, no consolation in any of these pagan belief systems which could offer comfort to a mother who had lost her son, or a husband who had lost his wife. They were without hope and without God in the world. (Ephesians 2:12).

How different was Paul's attitude to death, even his own death! He says, 'For me to live is Christ; to die is gain'. 'My desire is to depart and be with Christ for that is far better'. (Philippians 2:21,23). This is not some kind of Stoical disposition on Paul's part, but a looking forward to some future experience which will surpass in all its delight and intensity of joy all that has been his experience so far, even though his life is based on God-given grace and intimacy in the Holy Spirit. His hope is not built on some kind of philosophical speculation, but on an historical foundation, says Dr Morris. (Morris p 13). Paul says 'we believe that Jesus died and rose again; even so, through Jesus, God will bring with Him those who have fallen asleep. (1 Thessalonians 4:14).

This is also Paul's reasoning and logical deduction, that therefore, because of the historical and indisputable death and resurrection of Jesus, God will bring with Him through Jesus, those who are fallen asleep. Stott comments, If God did not abandon Jesus to death, He will not abandon the Christian to death either. (Stott p 98).

Paul does not speak of Jesus as of one who had fallen asleep. Jesus had deliberately taken upon Himself 'flesh and blood', because the ones whom He had come to save were of flesh and blood, and He wanted to be a partaker of the same nature with them. (Hebrews 2:14).

There was a reason for this. All human beings, creatures of flesh and blood, must die. They are all their lifetime subject to bondage, the bondage of the fear of death. Jesus could also die because He was also of flesh and blood. Though He was God, He had taken flesh and blood upon Himself so that He could offer Himself up as a perfect sacrifice to God on their behalf, for the forgiveness of their sins, which He could not do unless He was flesh and blood like themselves, (Hebrews 2:15).

But through the death of the Lord Jesus, through His human flesh, He had destroyed him who had the power of death, that is, the devil; and delivered all those who through fear of death were all their lifetime subject to bondage. (Hebrews 2:15)..
That sacrifice for sin had previously been the *continual offering* of sheep and goats. But Jesus, not through the blood of sheep and goats, but through His own blood entered the holy place *once and for all*, having obtained eternal redemption for us. (Hebrews 9:12).

Isaiah had said prophetically that the Lord will swallow up death forever, and He will wipe away tears from all faces.(Isaiah 25:8), and Paul is happy to conclude that with the death of the Lord Jesus, death is swallowed up in victory. (1 Corinthians 15:54).

He states triumphantly, 'O death, where is your victory? O death, where is your sting? The sting of death is sin and the power of sin is the law. But thanks be to God who gives us the victory through our Lord Jesus Christ'. (1 Corinthians 15:54-57). 'In all these things we are more than conquerors through Him that loved us'. (Romans 8:37).

Through His life, death and resurrection, Christ has fulfilled the law. It no longer has a hold on His redeemed sons and daughters. They are free from the law and the power of sin which is through the law. They are also free from the sting of death which is sin, for Christ has overcome death and bondage to the fear of death and in its place has given us life and immortality through the gospel. (2 Timothy 1:10).

Christ truly did not 'sleep' but 'die', and in His death accomplished the will of God which had been from before the foundation of the world. (1 Peter 1:20). But in His death He transformed death for us, not into some imagined horror, but into 'sleep'. And He rose again from the dead, demonstrating that the work had been done, demonstrating for all time and all eternity that death is dead, dealt with, abolished, extinguished for the believer. That as Christ has been raised from the dead, so will His children be. And until that time, they will walk in newness of life, to the glory of God the Father.

This is the triumph of the resurrection, God raising Him up from the dead because 'it is finished'. These are the words of the Lord Jesus as He hung on the cross. The work which Jesus came to do, He has fulfilled, accomplished. (John 19:30). 'It is finished'.

And when He comes, those who have 'fallen asleep in Jesus', died in Jesus, will God bring with Him. (1 Thessalonians 4:14). Paul is speaking of death through Jesus, and Bruce adds that death through Jesus is but the prelude to resurrection with Jesus. (Bruce, also quoting Morris, p 139).

1 Thessalonians 4: 15-18. The Coming Day.

For this we declare to you by the word of the Lord, that we who are alive, who are left until the coming of the Lord shall not precede those who have fallen asleep. For the Lord Himself will descend from heaven with a cry of command, with the archangel's call, and with the sound of the trumpet of God. And the dead in Christ will rise first; then we who are alive, who are left, shall be caught up together with them in the clouds, to meet the Lord in the air, and so we shall always be with the Lord. Therefore, comfort one another with these words. (1 Thessalonians 4:15-18).

Paul did not know whether he would still be alive at the coming of the Lord Jesus, but as he was expecting that at any time He would appear, he considered that he might possibly be among those who were witnesses of His coming. And that of course has been the expectation of all Christans since the Lord Jesus left the earth, the glorious expectation of His coming again to take His power and reign.

'Behold, He is coming with the clouds and every eye will see Him, and those who pierced Him, and all the tribes of the earth will mourn because of Him'. (Revelation 1:7). Not everyone will be glad to see Him for they will recognize that because of their sin He was pierced by the nails, and had the spear thrust through His side as He hung on the cross. But whether He is seen with the eye of joy or despair, with thankfulness or apprehension at the coming also of the day of judgement, He will come. And every eye will see Him.

Paul joyfully describes what will happen. The Lord Himself will appear in His full panoply as the Son of God, probably surrounded by the angelic host, all of them eager to catch a glimpse of all those faithful believers who have come out of the great tribulation, who have washed their robes and made them white in the blood of the Lamb. (Revelation 7:14). Then with what rejoicing will Jesus call to them and they will rise up to meet their Lord in the air. And so shall they be forever with the Lord.

This is a dramatic revelation. Even to think about His coming, to imagine what it will be like is stimulating and exciting; to know that the whole earth will be filled with the glory of God as the waters cover the sea, (Habakkuk 2:14). and all flesh shall see it together, for the mouth of the Lord has spoken it. (Isaiah 40:5).

Paul's description suggests that those who have died in Christ will the Lord bring with Him as He descends through the clouds. (1 Thessalonians 4:13). Since falling asleep they have been in heaven with Him and now when He comes back to the earth, they will come too. And those who are alive will be caught up together with them to meet the Lord in the air. Those who had formerly been asleep but are now raised from the dead are now with Jesus, all together with each other in what Stott calls 'the unbreakable solidarity which the people of Christ enjoy with Him and with each other. And which death is utterly unable to destroy'. (Stott p 98).

This is what Paul is declaring to the Thessalonians as 'the word of the Lord'. (1 Thessalonians 4:15). This is something which God has revealed to him and which he is holding in his heart for comfort, for he may have known some at least of those who had 'fallen asleep', as Stephen did after being stoned to death. (Acts 7:60). Paul describes himself as having been near death from the countless beatings he received. (2 Corinthians 11:23).

It is not beyond the bounds of credulity to suppose that many Christians as well as Stephen had been subjected to similar treatment as they were persecuted for the sake of the gospel, and Paul writes that the Thessalonians too had suffered much affliction. (1 Thessalonians 3:4). They had suffered the same things from their own countrymen as the churches of God had suffered in Judea from the Jews, who killed both the Lord Jesus, and the prophets, who had also been killed. (1 Thessalonians 2:14). There was a real atmosphere of antagonism in Thessalonica against the believers.

Paul is not writing from an aloof theological doctrine of eschatology. This is real to him, part of his own experience. He shared the suffering of the Thessalonians, their grief and their deep sorrow. But God had given him this tremendous hope, that those who had fallen asleep, either naturally or from persecution, his beloved brothers and sisters, Jesus would bring with Him when He returned. He longed to see the Lord Jesus. He longed to see Him reigning in glory, but he also longed to see those whom he had loved coming on the clouds of glory with Him and meeting them with his Lord in the air. Therefore, he concludes, comfort one another with these words. (1 Thessalonians 4:18). These are indeed comfortable words. He and they will always and forever be with the Lord.

Paul is expectant, waiting for the cry of the archangel, for the sound of the trumpet, the clarion call from God accompanied by the archangel's triumphant response, 'He is coming!', and the trumpet sound that no one could imitate, the universal note that everyone could hear, authoritatively announcing that a new era was beginning.

Those whom He loves will never be separated from the Lord. (Romans 8:38,39). Stott says, 'they died through Him, they sleep in Him, they will rise with Him, and they will come with Him too'. (1 Thessalonians 4:14-16). They belong to each other and to Him. These are comfortable words for the Thessalonians and for us, grounded not in optimism but in hope, and communicated to us on the authority of the Lord Himself. (1 Thessalonians 4:15. Bruce p 103).

He who testifies to these things, Jesus Himself, says 'Surely I am coming soon!'. Amen, come Lord Jesus. (Revelation 22:16,20).

1 Thessalonians Chapter 5

1 Thessalonians 5:1-11. Times and seasons.

But as to the times and seasons, brethren, you have no need to have anything written to you. For you yourselves know well that the day of the Lord will come like a thief in the night. When people say 'There is peace and security', then sudden destruction will come upon them as travail comes upon a woman with child. But you are not in darkness, brethren, for that day to surprise you like a thief. For you are all sons of light and sons of the day; we are not of the night or of darkness. (1 Thessalonians 5:1-5)

Paul has a caveat. How wonderful it will be, the Thessalonians may have thought, to relax and wait as they listen for the sound of the trumpet; for they know the day of His coming will be a day of deep joy. We shall see Jesus! they may have thought. We shall be united with all those whom we have loved and lost for a while. A glorious day is coming and coming soon! But Paul says, 'As to times and seasons brethren, as to the *chronos* and the *kairos,* you know that the day of the Lord will come as a thief in the night. (1 Thessalonians 5:2). Suddenly, unexpectedly, He will be here. And it will be a terrible day for some.

When people are saying comfortably to themselves, this is a time of peace and security, then sudden destruction will come upon them. It will be as when a woman gives birth. Suddenly she is in labour. She knew that the time of delivery was drawing near, but she does not know when the pains of childbirth will suddenly come upon her, and she cannot escape the pain until the child is born. (1 Thessalonians 5:3). When the Lord comes, there will be no escape from the sudden destruction which will come upon the earth, a concept which Paul amplifies in 2 Thessalonians as the punishment of eternal destruction and exclusion from the presence of the Lord and from the glory of His might. (2 Thessalonians 1:9).

How the believers in Thessalonica longed to see Him! But they had to recognize that God's times and seasons are not necessarily coincident with ours. He will come in his own appointed time. Like you, says Paul, we long for Him. Together we wait for Him. We are children of light, not children of darkness, and the light cannot be manufactured; it is a gift from the Lord Jesus who said 'he who follows Me shall not walk in darkness but shall have the light of life. (John 8:12). He is the light of the world. There is no darkness in Him. (1 John 1:5). If we walk in fellowship with Him, in His light, with His transparency, we walk in the light.

But there are those whom the coming day will reveal as children of darkness. The day of the Lord casts its radiance before and throws up in sharp relief those who are 'not of the day but of the night'. (1 Thessalonians 5:5). The children of darkness are those for whom we should, and do, pray and to whom we should witness of the love of the Lord for them; and seek to encourage them to come to Him for grace and forgiveness.

There is a sense in which they are asleep, says Paul, unaware of the tremendous purpose of God for His new creation, the church. God called the light out of darkness at the beginning of the creation of the world, (Genesis 1:3) for He wanted His children to live in the light, and that means being awake, and not asleep to all that He is doing. Now God has sent Jesus, the light of the world, (John 8:12), and His children are patiently waiting for Him to work His work of grace in human hearts. So, the believers must clothe themselves with sobriety and not with drunkenness, 'and let us not sleep as others do, but let us keep awake and be sober', says Paul. (1 Thessalonians 5:6).

And in addition, Paul says, let us put on the breastplate of faith and love to protect our hearts, and for a helmet let us put on the hope of salvation to guard our minds, (1 Thessalonians 5:8), as soldiers in the infantry of God, waiting upon our Captain's word of command.

In His great love, God had provided salvation for all people through the Lord Jesus Christ. (1 Thessalonians 5:9). But He had given men and women free will and some received His salvation gladly, and some rejected it. They preferred the darkness to the light, and some of the activities that were performed in the darkness caused God to impose His judgement on them. For those who received Him, whether engaged in normal sleep or normal wakefulness, their life was in Him. For God has not destined us for wrath, or judgement, but to obtain salvation through our Lord Jesus Christ, who died for us, so whether we wake or sleep, we might live with Him. (1 Thessalonians 5:10).

How important therefore, to encourage one another and build one another up in our life in Him, as Paul is convinced the Thessalonians are doing. There is darkness and there is light, and the Thessalonian believers are all sons of the light and of the day. (1 Thessalonians 5:5). There is sleep and there is wakefulness, alertness, and Paul is encouraging his brothers and sisters to be alert, to be awake for the coming of the Lord. There is drunkenness and there is sobriety and Paul explains that so often, darkness and drunkenness go together. (1 Thessalonians 5:7). But since these believers belong to the day, to the light, they will be sober. The question is, what will Jesus expect them to be doing when He comes?

Paul is pointing out the divisiveness which the gospel creates; humanity is divided even as the cosmos is divided, day and night. He is saying that there is a vast spiritual contrast between the followers of Jesus, and those who are ignorant of Him, or reject Him.

Paul describes this condition in 2 Corinthians 4:4 as 'the god of this world having blinded the minds of unbelievers, to keep them from seeing the light of the gospel of the glory of God in the face of Jesus Christ who is the likeness of God, the very image of God'. But God said, 'let light shine out of darkness', and He has shone in our hearts to give us the light of the knowledge of the glory of God in the face of Jesus Christ'. We live in the light of the glory of God reflected from the face of Jesus.

And one day, the light of the glory of God will split the universe asunder as the Lord Jesus returns in all His glory to take His people to Himself.

There are times and seasons. (1 Thessalonians 5:5). In Greek there are two words for time.There is a *waiting* time, *chronos, the time in which we live* and in which God is *moving towards the time* appointed by Him when the trumpet will sound; when there will be no more delay. (Revelation 10:6). Then will come the *kairos* time, the time of *the consummation* of all things, *the event* when suddenly, all the anticipation will be realized, when God has moved through history to complete the history of His world, when *chronos* time will have come to an end.

During the time of waiting, those who have been enlightened may taste the powers of the age to come. (Hebrews 6:15). They are anticipating the glory that will be revealed, the revelation of the sons of God as the creation is set free from its bondage to decay and they obtain the glorious liberty of the children of God. (Romans 8:18-23). But Paul says, they also groan inwardly as they wait in hope for what they do not yet see. They wait in patience for it, believing that in everything God works for good with those who love Him (Romans 8:28).

So the two concepts of *chronos* and *kairos*, of constant patient waiting and sudden glorious event, the times and the seasons, come together. It is a constant theme throughout the New Testament, the *not yet* and the *now.*

Jesus said, 'He who believes in the Son *has* eternal life', with the very real implication that he or she has it *now,* as he or she believes. (John 3:36). But at the grave of Lazarus, Jesus said to Martha that He is the resurrection and the life, as she grieved for the death of her beloved brother. And Jesus did not correct her or rebuke her when she went beyond His statement to suggest that her brother would have eternal life even more fully at the resurrection, at the last day.. The last day is when the perishable nature must put on imperishability, and the mortal nature must put on immortality, at the sounding of the trumpet. (1 Corinthians 15:53).

Paul claims that our citizenship is in heaven and from it we wait for a Saviour, the Lord Jesus Christ, who will change our lowly body, that it might be like His glorious body, by the power by which He is able to subdue all things to Himself. (Philippians 3:20). Christ is on his way, and we wait in anticipation of the glory that shall be revealed.

1 Thessalonians 5:11-14. The fellowship of the church.

Therefore, encourage one another and build one another up, just as you are doing. But we beseech you brethren, to respect those who labour over you in the Lord, to esteem them very highly in love because of their work. Be at peace among yourselves; and we exhort you brethren, admonish the idlers; encourage the fainthearted; help the weak; be patient with them all. (1 Thessalonians 5:11-14).

Therefore, Paul says, encourage one another and build one another up. Strengthen one another, help each other to grow spiritually, just as you are doing. This is the conclusion he draws from the promise of the Lord's coming. Bruce says, the eschatalogical hope is not an excuse for idling, but an incentive for action, and especially for mutual aid. Every church member has a duty to help in building up the community so that it may attain spiritual maturity. (Bruce p 115). There are those among them who labour in the gospel. Paul encourages the believers to respect them and to esteem them very highly in love because of their work. (1 Thessalonians 5:12,13)

Wanamaker suggests that Paul had a particular concern that all members of the community had a mutual responsibility to help each other as they carry out the demands of their faith and especially towards those who communicate the theological concepts underlying those demands. (Wanamaker p 190).

Paul recognizes five basic area of concern; recognition and respect for *leaders,* (1 Thessalonians 5:12-13), encouragement for the *idlers,* those who are out of step as a soldier might be, (1 Thessalonians 5:14); tenderness towards the *fainthearted,* the discouraged, (1 Thessalonians 5:14); help for the *weak,* to hold them as they cling to them, to put their arms around them, (Stott p 122; Barclay p 240); and to be *patient with all,* (1 Thessalonians 5:14). just as we so often need the Lord to be patient with us.

1 Thessalonians 5:16-22. Worship in the church.

Rejoice always, pray constantly, give thanks in all circumstances, for this the will of God concerning you. Do not quench the Spirit. Do not despise prophesying but test everything; hold fast that which is good; abstain from every form of evil. (1 Thessalonians 5:16-22).

This is a community of reciprocal love, of mutual support, of the encouragement of one another, especially of those with a special need of encouragement. If the community are at peace among themselves, there will be no envy of one another, no need to repay an insult with an even more hurtful comment. Revenge, recrimination, retaliation are unknown in such a community which is always seeking the good of the other.

In such a fellowship of love it is possible to rejoice always, pray constantly, give thanks in all circumstances, knowing that 'this is the will of God concerning you'. (1 Thessalonians 5:16-!8). Barclay writes, 'they pray together best who also pray alone'. (Barclay p 240). When believers are privately and individually living a life of rejoicing in the Lord, of constant prayer and heartfelt recognition of the provision of all the blessings showered upon them, it must overflow into the times when they meet together. Barclay says that this is what makes a happy and thankful church. (Barclay p 240).

But how does a Christian believer, or even more, a Christain community, achieve such a goal? Must it always be just an aspiration?

Paul is emphatic. He says 'quench not the Spirit'.(1 Thessalonians 5:19). Individually, as they walk with the Lord, as they live in the Spirit, they are aware of His guidance. Through the work of the Holy Spirit they have come into a life lived in the joy of being a follower of the Lord Jesus, of belonging to Him and whatever the circumstances, of being constantly prayerful as they live in fellowship and perfect dependence on Him. They know that they are in the will of their loving heavenly Father and that all things are governed by his will. (1 Thessalonians 5:18), so that in everything they can give thanks, for what they cannot see of His will for them, they know He can see, and can provide the peace in their hearts that nothing can take away. (1 Thessalonians 5:23).

How wonderful is such a life, lived in the Spirit, trusting the Lord. But Paul has an even more wonderful way of living the Christian life. He says, *'We exhort you brethren, we urge you* that you admonish the unruly, encourage the fainthearted, help the weak, be patient with everyone, that none of you repays evil for evil but seek to do good to one another and to all, and rejoice always. (1 Thessalonians 5:14). Paul is speaking to all the brethren, to all his brothers and sisters, to the whole church.

It is also as the church together that they rejoice in the goodness of the Lord and praise Him. It is as the church together that they pray constantly. It is as the church that they give thanks for all that the Holy Spirit Is doing amongst them. They must not quench the Holy Spirit. And when they come together, they must not despise prophetic utterances, but examine everything carefully; they must hold fast to that which is good and abstain from every appearance of evil.

How important is the presence and activity of the Holy Spirit as the church meets together. How dangerous for them to quench the power of the Holy Spirit in their midst; to attempt to extinguish His presence; to attempt to function as a church without Him. He must be allowed, entreated to have His way, for we cannot impose boundaries, limitations on God. We must acknowledge His sovereignty and respond to all that He is saying or doing. The alternative is that our very identity as the people of God is brought into question.

1 Thessalonians 5:23-24. Sanctification.

Now may the God of peace Himself sanctify you entirely. And may your spirit, soul and body be preserved completely without blame at the coming of our Lord Jesus Christ. Faithful is He who called you, who also will do it. (1 Thessalonians 5:23, 24).

Paul returns to the theme of sanctification, for after all, the church is composed of those who are sanctified, called 'saints', separated from the world; separated and set apart for God. Paul has returned to the personal, the individual. He says, may the God of peace Himself sanctify you wholly, and may your spirit, soul and body be preserved blameless at the coming of our Lord Jesus Christ.

Not only in our church life but as we individually seek to follow the Lord, we need to hear Paul's injunction again. 'Do not grieve the Spirit', for He is the agent of sanctification. (1 Thessalonians 4:18). He is the One who will keep us sound and blameless in spirit, soul and body at the coming of the Lord Jesus, for He is also the God of peace. (1 Thessalonians 5:23). We may look at ourselves and really question how far we have come, to what degree have we been sanctified for we know our hearts. But we look away to Jesus and know that He has called us. He has called us into sanctification, (1 Corinthians 1:2), to the ongoing experience of becoming more like Him.

God desires a people who are completely devoted to Him. This is what He has called us to. Paul assures the Thessalonian believers, 'He who called you is faithful, and He will do it'. (1 Thessalonians 5:24). The God of peace, the Holy Spirit and the Lord Jesus Christ are all engaged in keeping blameless the whole, entire person of the believer until the coming of the Lord Jesus; the whole spirit, soul and body of the one who has been called by Him. This is amazing, almost incredible. Can we really believe this? Do we not say with the Psalmist, 'It is high, I cannot attain unto it. (Psalm 139:4). Yes, it is really true. The word of God says it and we believe it. God is faithful and He will do it.

The faithfulness of God is the theme of the whole Bible. Leon Morris writes (p 184), 'in the last resort, what matters most is not the believer's hold of God, but God's strong grip on him'. But the process is not yet complete. Paul is aware of this. He has already told the Thessalonians how earnestly he prays for them, (1 Thessalonians 3:18). Now He asks them to pray for him and 'for us'. (1 Thessalonians 5:25). He is not setting himself above these precious believers, he is asking for their prayers, for himself and Silas and Timothy too. We lift one another up to the Lord in prayer, loving one another as we love the Lord, and when we are together, greet one another with a holy kiss. (1 Thessalonians 5:26).

The love which Christians feel for each other is not a remote spiritual emotion but a personal and physical expression of an inner reality; of a bond which unites them, a holy eucharistic kiss of thanksgiving for each other. One cannot kiss another with hostility in one's heart, and one cannot kiss another from a distance.

The greeting of one another in this way is an almost instinctive, automatic response to one another in love. The bond of fellowship between believers is greater than any other kind of bond except the marriage bond, the reaching out to one another in love because they both love the same Lord.

It has been said that when meeting someone for the first time, it is easy to see at once if they are a lover of the Lord Jesus for there is a distinct family likeness. We are brothers and sisters, children of the same heavenly Father. We are the family of God. How can we help but love one another and demonstrate that love physically with a holy kiss? Here, in 1 Thessalonians 5:26. and also in Romans 16:16 and 2 Corinthians 13:12, Paul has given us permission to do so, as has Peter in his first letter, (1 Peter 5:14), indicating that this may have been a common practice in the early church.

In effect, Paul is saying to his beloved Thessalonians, 'how I long to see you and greet you with a loving kiss!' They had become very dear to him. He is sending affectionate greetings to each one, these men and women whom he has come to love, all the 'brethren', those who are weak or might have come adrift from the fellowship, all those who needed comfort or encouragement. Paul is sending his love to them all.

Paul has come to the end of his letter, but he realizes that the church in Thessalonica is only a small part of what God is doing throughout Macedonia, so he makes one last request. He says, 'I adjure you by the Lord that this letter be read by *all the brethren*'. (1 Thessalonians 5:27). Paul had been conscious while writing this letter of the inspiration of the Holy Spirit. HIs teaching about the coming of the Lord is specifically mentioned as being 'the word of the Lord'. (1 Thessalonians 4:15), and there is no doubt that both he and they would have viewed what had been revealed to him as coming from the Holy Spirit.

Paul's letters had not yet been understood as being canonical, that is, accepted as sacred scripture, as they afterwards were, but Paul did know that what he had written was an important continuation of what he and Silas and Timothy had been preaching and teaching while still with them. This was so important that Paul was 'adjuring' them, charging them solemnly to share the letter 'with *all* the brethren'. (1 Thessalonians 5:27). Not one church, not one believer should be excluded. The content and implication of all that Paul had written was to be made available to all because it had come from the Holy Spirit through Paul.

Paul wanted to make sure that 'all' of the brethren, perhaps those who had been away on business, or had been ill at home, or for some other reason could not join with their brothers and sisters in worship, 'those who were far off and those who were near', (to borrow a phrase used in a different though related context, Ephesians 2:17); all should have the privilege of hearing what the Spirit was saying to the churches. (Revelation 2:7,11,17). It is totally conceivable that those Thessalonians with the skill to copy the letter would immediately retrieve their stylus, inkhorn, penknife and scroll of parchment to obey Paul's injunction. (Jeremiah 8:8; 36:23; Ezra 9:2).

As we hold in our hands this sacred text, we are grateful to all those who heeded Paul's request, both then and subsequently, the preservation of the word of God.

I Thessalonians 5:25-28. The final benediction.

The grace of our Lord Jesus Christ be with you.

Paul ends his letter as he began. He began, 'grace and peace be with you', (1 Thessalonians 1:1). He ends, 'the grace of the Lord Jesus Christ be with you'. God is unchanging in His love for us; His constant loving care most especially necessary when we deserve it least.

It is difficult to define grace. Some have expressed it quite neatly as God's Riches At Christ's Expense, but this is not altogether satisfying. We somehow feel there is more to grace even than that, though we do recognize the tremendous cost of our salvation. Stott, along with many others, calls it 'the unmerited favour of God'. He continues, 'for Paul to end with grace is no empty conventional formula, for grace is at the heart of the gospel. It is indeed the heart of God. (Stott p 135).

According to Wanamaker, the profound theological conviction of the early church is reflected in the language used by Paul, that Jesus Christ was the source of divine grace, that is, the totality of salvation for those who confess Him as Lord. (Wanamaker quoting Conzelmann p 209).

Leon Morris believes that this is not just a greeting from Paul to his beloved brothers and sisters, but a prayer for them that they might know the grace of our Lord Jesus Christ. Morris quotes Denney as writing 'whatever God has to say to us begins and ends with grace. All that God has been to man is summed up in grace; all His gentleness and beauty, all His tenderness and patience, all the holy passion of His love. What more could any soul wish for another than that the grace of the Lord Jesus Christ should be with them?' (Morris quoting J.Denney. *The first and second epistles to the Thessalonians. London 1872*).

All loving concern originates with God and is in no way dependent on the intrinsic worth of the recipient. Grace defines God's love in utterly self giving terms. It is beyond logical analysis. But those who live in the grace of the Lord Jesus Christ have the confident assurance of certainty and spiritual security, and that even their faithlessness could not threaten the destruction of the grace of God to them. God is constantly faithful to the relationship for which He has provided. He is constantly steadfast in His grace towards His children whatever they are undergoing in terms of adversity, as Paul himself had found. Through his 'thorn in the flesh', Paul had discovered the all-sufficiency of the grace of Christ. (2 Corinthians 12:9). God *is* grace. Grace is the sheer self giving love of God towards men and women. (Wayne E. Ward. *The Lutterworth Dictionary of the Bible.* Cambridge 1994).

Through the grace of Christ, we are called to Him. (Galatians 1:6) His kindness, forbearance and patience, are elements of and expressions of His grace, and lead us to repentance. (Romans 2:4). And Paul says through His grace He has saved us, the immeasurable riches of His grace in kindness towards us in Christ Jesus. Paul repeats, ' By grace you have been saved, through faith, and this is not of yourselves, it is the gift of God'. (Epesians 2:7-9). And further, 'by grace we have been justified in His sight as a gift through the redemption which is in Christ Jesus'. (Romans 3:23).

We owe everything to God's grace. Grace is the kindness of God to us. Through every daily circumstance we know, we feel His surrounding, supporting kindness towards us.

Grace and truth came by Jesus Christ, were incarnated in Jesus. (John 1:14). Grace and truth came to us who were disobedient, rebels from the grace of God but were brought near to the One who had destined us in love to be His sons according to the riches of His grace which He freely bestowed on us in the Beloved, so that we might live to the praise of the glory of His grace. (Ephesians 1:5-8). And it is by His grace, and only by His grace, His everlasting kindness and love towards us that we may and will live in His grace.

So Paul can prayerfully say. 'The grace of the Lord Jesus Christ be with you'. His amazing grace. And we would add, Amen.

Dr Moffatt writes, the religion of the Bible is a religion of grace or it is nothing. No grace, no gospel. (Moffat. *Grace in the New Testament* 1931 p 15).

The Second Letter of Paul to the Thessalonians

Introduction

Paul, Silvanus and Timothy to the church of the Thessalonians in God the Father and the Lord Jesus Christ. Grace to you and peace from God the Father and the Lord Jesus Christ. (2 Thessalonians 1:1-2)

From Paul's first letter to the Thessalonians and the further account in Acts 16:1-6, we understand that Paul and Silas (called Silvanus in the Pauline letters) set out on what is traditionally described as Paul's second missionary journey after the Council of Jerusalem in Acts 15:5-29. The reference to the emperor Claudius, 44-49 A.D. in Acts 18:2 would indicate that the missionaries arrived in Thessalonica in about 49 A.D., less than twenty years after the death and resurrection of the Lord Jesus.

Accompanied by Timothy, who had joined them at Lystra, they travelled northward through Asia until they reached Troas, a northern port on the Aegean Sea, where they were joined by Luke. (Acts 16:3,10). Paul's vision of the man from Macedonia, and his entreaty to them to 'Come over to Macedonia and help us', (Acts 16 9), caused them to cross the Aegean Sea into Macedonia, northern Greece. They travelled along the Via Egnatia until they came to Philippi where after preaching the gospel, Paul and Sias were brutally beaten and incarcerated in prison, from which they were released after an earthquake had opened all the prison doors. (Acts 16:26). On being pleaded with by the authorities to leave Philippi, they continued on their journey along the Via Egnatia until they reached Thessalonica, about ninety miles from Philippi. (Acts 17:1).

Paul's custom was always to take the gospel message to the synagogue first, and this he did in Thessalonica; and after only three weeks, there was a considerable body of believers in Thessalonica, including Greeks, and not a few of the leading women, who had turned from paganism, from idols, to serve the living and true God and to wait for His Son from heaven. (Acts 17:4; I Thessalonians 1:9,10).

But jealousy of the teaching of Paul and Silas caused the Jews to stage a riot, press ganging some 'lewd fellows of the baser sort', (K.J.V), into setting the city into an uproar. (Acts 17:5). Paul and Silas were quietly escorted to Beroea from where Paul was then conducted to Athens when similar riots broke out in Beroea. (Acts 17:15). After preaching in Athens, Paul went to Corinth in Achaia, southern Greece. The emperor Claudius had issued an edict compelling all Jews to leave Rome, and in Corinth Paul found Priscilla and Aquila, exiles from Rome, and stayed with them, for they were tentmakers.

Silas and Timothy eventually arrived in Corinth from Macedonia, (Acts 18:5),and Paul stayed in Corinth for eighteen months, teaching the word of God among them. (Acts 18:11).

Since the edict from Claudius was delivered in 49 A.D. it is possible to date the time when Paul was in Corinth, and since Silas and Timothy, co-authors of the letters to the Thessalonians (1 Thessalonians 1:1; 2 Thessalonians 1:1) were also in Corinth at that time, it is legitimate to conclude that the letters to the Thessalonians were written from Corinth by Paul, Silvanus and Timothy between 49 and 51 A.D.

2 Thessalonians 1:1-3. The authors of the letter.

Paul, Silvanus and Timothy, to the church of the Thessalonians in God the Father and the Lord Jesus Christ. Grace to you and peace from God the Father and the Lord Jesus Christ. (2THessalonians 1:1,2).

In each of these letters to the Thessalonians, Paul, Silvanus and Timothy are named as joint authors. Timothy is also named along with Paul in others of the Pauline corpus, (2 Corinthians, Philippians, Colossians, Philemon) because he was with Paul when they were written.

Silas had a more independent status as being one of the leading men 'among the brethren' in the council of Jerusalem, (Acts 15:22), but was a loyal and trustworthy colleague of Paul's as they visited the churches in the cities of Asia Minor. (Acts 16:4). They had suffered together, sung hymns together and prayed together (Acts 16:25), and rejoiced together over the newly established community of believers in Philippi. Silas had been in danger together with Paul from the opposition of the Jews in both Thessalonica and Beroea, and Silas and Timothy had stayed in Macedonia, without doubt encouraging the new believers, while Paul was temporarily stranded in Athens.

Both of these letters to the Thessalonians begin with thanksgiving for the Thessalonian believers. In the first letter, Paul writes, 'we give thanks to God always for you all'. (1 Thessalonians 1:2). There is an added emphasis in 2 Thessalonians 1:3. Paul says 'we are *bound* to give thanks always for you all'. Paul, Silas and Timothy are united in saying that we cannot help but thank God always for you all; it is our duty and our joy because we are so greatly encouraged by your increasing faith and love, reported to us so recently when Timothy returned to us from his visit to you. (1 Thessalonians 3:6).

Paul and Silas and Timothy had prayed earnestly, night and day that they might see the face of these beloved believers, (1 Thessalonians 3:10), but it was not until five years afterwards that this prayer was answered and Paul was able to revisit Macedonia.

Bruce writes, 'towards the end of Paul's Ephesian ministry, in the spring of 55 A.D., he planned to pass through Macedonia on his way to Corinth, (1 Corinthians 16:5; 2 Corinthians 1:15). Though because of certain problems in Corinth, he was obliged to change his plans as far as Corinth was concerned, (2 Corinthian 1:23), he was able to make another visit to Macedonia, (Acts 19:21, 20:1). Bruce suggests that a careful reading of the evidence would show that his stay in the province of Macedonia, which of course included Philippi and Beroea as well as Thessalonica, was longer than might have appeared on the surface of Acts; that Paul had been able to travel further along the Via Egnatia than had been possible on his first visit. (Bruce p xxvii).

Paul and Timothy had not only prayed to be able to see the faces of the believers, but also to supply what was lacking in their faith. (1 Thessalonians 3:10). This prayer was also answered but more immediately. Now they are bound to give thanks for answered prayer because the faith of these dear Thessalonians is growing abundantly and the love of every one of them is increasing. (2 Thessalonians 1:3).

Paul becomes exuberant as he thinks of them. In his greeting to them in his first letter he had written 'grace to you and peace' which was not only a greeting or a conventional way of opening a letter, but a prayer; grace, the unmerited favour of God to them, and peace, resting in the love of God as they trusted Him. But in this second letter, Paul has expanded his greeting, or more probably, his prayer for them.

He writes, grace to you and peace *from God the Father and the Lord Jesus Christ.* Bruce comments, the spontaneous joining together of God the Father and the Lord Jesus Christ under a single preposition bears witness to the exalted place which the risen Christ occupies in the thought of Paul and his colleagues. Christ has been invested by God with the title *kyrios, (Gk),* Lord, the name which is above every name, that at the name of Jesus every knee shall bow and every tongue confess that *He is LORD,* to the glory of God the Father. (Philippians 2:10,11). God and Christ are entirely at one, both in the salvation of believers, and as together they maintain a spiritual fellowship. (Bruce p 7).

Paul's affection for the brethren, his brothers and sisters in Christ, has increased more and more, and we may assume the affection of Silas and Timothy for them as well, as they witness to the faith of the believers growing abundantly, 'and the love of every one of you for one another increasing'. (2 Thessalonians 1:3).

2 Thessalonians 2:1,2. The occasion for the letter.

Now concerning the coming of our Lord Jesus Christ and our assembling to meet Him, we beg you, brethren, not to be quickly shaken in mind, or excited either by spirit or word or by letter purporting to be from us to the effect that the day of the Lord has come.

It is generally accepted that both Thessalonian letters were written from Corinth shortly after Paul and his colleagues had arrived there, about 50 A.D. (though some theologians hold alternative views), and we assume that the same recipients are being addressed.

The first letter had been written primarily to encourage the believers to stand firm under affliction and to increase in their faith more and more, and also secondly, to put their minds at rest over what would happen to their friends who had 'fallen asleep', when the Lord Jesus came again at His *parousia*, His second coming. (1 Thessalonians 4:13).

The first letter had been sent out with prayer. The concerns of the Thessalonian community had been the earnest object of prayer, and Paul and his companions were overwhelmed in their thanksgiving to God that prayer had been answered. In this second letter, Paul is having to use superlatives to express his gratitude to God for their super abundant faith, for their ever increasing love for one another in spite of all the affliction they continued to experience, their suffering for the kingdom of God. (2 Thessalonians 1:3-5).

The first letter to the Thesalonians had been written after Timothy had reported back to Paul and Silas in Corinth, not long after Paul had left Thessalonica. (1 Thessalonians 2:17). Paul had sent Timothy to Thessalonica from Athens, (1 Thessalonians 3:1,2), so we would have expected that Timothy would rejoin Paul in Athens, but it appears that Timothy may have gone straight to Corinth on learning that Paul was now there, for we also learn that Timothy joined Paul in Corinth. (Acts 18:5). It is more likely that this letter was written from Corinth than from Athens, where Paul stayed for a very short time, especially since the situation concerning those who had 'fallen asleep' may have taken time to develop. (1 Thessalonians 4:13). Paul had also encouraged the Thessalonian believers to live quietly, to mind their own affairs and to work with their hands, (1 Thessalonians 4:10), and this took time, convinced as they were of the Lord's near return while pursuing a normal lifestyle.

Another factor could be that there is no record in Acts of Silas working together with Paul after Acts 18:5., although both letters to the Thessalonians employ the name of Silvanus as joint author.

Our conclusion is that Paul, Silvanus (Silas), and Timothy co-authored 1 Thessalonians from Corinth, and shortly afterwards, 2 Thessalonians too. There is every indication that 2 Thessalonians was written only weeks after 1 Thessalonians. The same sort of situation had arisen in Thessalonica, although the Thessalonian preoccupation with the *parousia,* the second coming of Christ, had now been complicated by the assertion of some that that the day of the Lord, the day of His coming, has already taken place.

2 Thessalonians Chapter 1

2 Thessalonians 1:3-5. Thanksgiving for the believers.

We are bound to give thanks always for you brethren, as is fitting, because your faith is growing abundantly and the love for one another is increasing. Therefore we ourselves boast of you in the churches of God for your steadfastness and faith in all your persecutions and in the afflictions which you are enduring. (2 Thessalonians 1:3,4).

Opposition from unbelievers is difficult, and the faithful Thessalonians had already suffered much at the hands of those who would attempt to destroy them as witnesses to the gospel of Christ. But this further attack, from those who were presumably believers, who would deceive them about the coming of the Lord was probably harder to bear. How they longed for Paul or Silas to explain events more clearly for them. These deceivers had even sent a letter to them purporting to come from their beloved teachers to the effect that the day of the Lord had already come. Paul, Silas and Timothy were full of concern for the troubled Thessalonian believers when they heard this.

So there are these two issues for which the Thessalonians need encouragement. First, Paul wants them to see their suffering as God sees it, and secondly to assure them that Jesus had not yet returned to the earth.

Paul had occasion to boast of these beloved brothers and sisters to other churches of God, a boasting not of self congratulation as though it was due to the ministry of himself and Silas, but a boasting of what God had done in their lives; because their faith was growing abundantly and the love for each other was increasing while their steadfastness and faith were being tested by the persecution and affliction they were enduring. (2 Thessalonians 1:3,4).

Paul says 'we are bound to give thanks for you'. We cannot help it. God has done so much in you. In telling them of his boasting of them to the other Macedonian churches he is encouraging them, for Paul can see what they probably could not see as they endured the trials laid upon them, that those very trials are causing them to lean more and more heavily on the grace of God to them, more and more steadfastly on His unchanging love surrounding and supporting them, even reaching out to those who are persecuting them. But Paul could also perceive that the affliction which they are suffering had rebounded on to those who had caused the suffering. (2 Thessalonians 1:6). This is the judgement of God, evidence of His righteous judgement. (2 Thessalonians 1:5).

It could be that the Thessalonians considered themselves to be unworthy of Paul's assessment of their progress in the gospel, (2 Thessalonians 1:5) but Paul's assessment of their progress in spite of affliction is evidence of the righteous judgement of God, a true assessment of what God is doing in them; and he is 'bound to give thanks to God always for them. And he not only wants to give thanks, he feels compelled to do so, for he is deeply aware of God's validating of his own ministry among them, but more especially how God can work among people so lately addicted to Idolatry, but who had turned from idols to serve the living and true God, and to wait for His Son from heaven. (1 Thessalonians 1:9,10).

That these same people, men and women, could come to increasing faith in God and abundant love for one another is an indication that God is among them indeed, and on this note of extreme gratitude, and praise to God, Paul gives thanks for them. As Paul is always praying and giving thanks for them, so they are growing in faith and love. (2 Thessalonians 1:3).

This is the faith they refuse to renounce in spite of persecution. Paul does not specify what is the character of these persecutions, preferring to concentrate on the faith of the believers under persecution, but as he himself had suffered at the hands of the 'jealous Jews' in Thessalonica we are given some idea. (Acts 17:5).

The initial period of opposition may well have become intensified after Paul had left Thessalonica and perhaps it is for this reason that Paul had sent faithful Timothy to them, 'to establish you in your faith and to exhort you, to encourage you, that no-one be moved by these afflictions'. (1 Thessalonians 3:12). Those who afflict God's people will also suffer affliction, (2 Thessalonians 1:6), and what is even more terrible, will pay the penalty of having to be shut out from the presence of the Lord and from the glory of His power when He comes to be glorified in His saints. (2 Thessalonians 1:9,10).

These afflictions may be a continuation of what had gone before, or there may be a different dimension to their suffering for which Paul is concerned in this second letter. It was the prospect, the hope of the Lord's near return which had given them the strength to endure. But if, as those who had written these false letters to them had claimed, the Lord had come and they had not seen His face or been taken up to meet Him in the air as Paul had promised would certainly be the case, what was the purpose and point of going on?

In his first letter to them, Paul had described the coming of the day of the Lord in glowing terms. The Thessalonian believers did not need to grieve for those who had 'fallen asleep' as those who had no hope. It was quite legitimate to grieve the loss of these dear ones, those who had been so precious to them. Paul had assured them, with all the certainty of which he was capable, that when Jesus came again, He would bring with Him all those precious believers. The Lord Himself would descend from heaven with a cry of command, with the voice of the archangel, and with the sound of the trumpet of God. The volume of noise would be unmistakable, completely unmissable, though surely harmonious and in no way excruciating, glorifying God. And the dead in Christ would rise first, then we who are alive, who are left, will be raptured, caught up to meet the Lord in the air. And so shall we ever be with the Lord.

This was the word of the Lord to Paul. (1 Thessalonians 4:15). This was what Paul himself was looking forward to. It was giving him comfort and strength and he believed that it would also comfort them. Therefore he says, comfort one another with these words. (1 Thessalonians 4:18). But there is a darker side which Paul had not disclosed in his first letter.

2 Thessalonians 1:6-12. The revelation of the Lord Jesus Christ from heaven.

For God deems it just to repay with affliction those who afflict you, and to grant rest, with us, to you who are afflicted, when the Lord Jesus is revealed from heaven with His mighty angels in flaming fire, inflicting vengeance upon those who do not obey the gospel of our Lord Jesus. (2 Thessalonians 1:6-8).

Paul says there is a principle here. God is just. His judgement is just. And as it is a righteous activity of God to provide men and women with salvation through the death of His Son, so it is just and righteous to bring punishment to those who persist in doing evil, 'to repay with affliction' those who afflict the suffering believers. (2 Thessalonians 1:6).

This is the time of the justice, the righteous judgement of God, and the persecution of the believers is evidence that they are being made worthy of the kingdom of God. (2 Thessalonians 1:5). God needs people whose lives are 'reigning' with Him, in total alignment with His will, who will be what He intended them to be, a royal priesthood, a holy nation, God's own people, a people for His own possession, declaring the wonderful deeds of Him who called them out of darkness into His wonderful light. (1 Peter 2:9). Their persecution, their suffering, to which they could put an end if they renounced their faith, is evidence of His righteous judgement, that they are worthy of the kingdom of God, worthy to suffer for His sake. (Bruce p 149; Morris p 199).

Stott comments that on the Thessalonians' success, instead of flattering them, Paul thanked God for the evidence of His *grace*. And In their sufferings, instead of complaining, Paul thanked God for the evidence of His *justice*. (Stott p 147). The suffering of the Thessalonians, the result of the behaviour of their enemies against them, has to come under the judgement of God; but there is a compensating factor as well for the believers. God Himself will grant rest, relief to the afflicted ones when the Lord Jesus will be revealed from heaven with His mighty angels in flaming fire. (2 Thessalonians 1:7). Paul says that God will grant His rest to them 'with us', for he himself knows what it means to suffer for the sake of Christ. (1 Corinthians 4:9-13; 2 Corinthians 6:4-10; 11:23-33).

In Philippians 3:10. Paul writes of his desire to be conformed to the death of Christ, to share the fellowship of His sufferings, to enter into that supreme love which is priceless but free, throwing away what is refuse, to gain that which is without price, knowing Christ and the power of His resurrection. (Philippians 3:8,10).

Since this is Paul's estimate of what it means to suffer, to count everything as loss because of the surpassing worth of knowing Christ Jesus his Lord, and for His sake to have suffered the loss of all things, to count them as refuse in order that he may gain Christ; he must regard the sufferings of the Thessalonians as a privilege. They suffer with Him in order that they may also be glorified with Him. (Romans 8:17).

But Paul also knows that God is righteous, and that retribution has to take place. When the Lord Jesus is revealed from heaven will be the time of God's vengeance upon those who do not obey the gospel of the Lord Jesus. (2 Thessalonians 1:7,8). These will pay the penalty of eternal destruction, away from the presence of the Lord and from the glory of His power. Now He is hidden from the world, but the day of His revelation is coming, His *apocalypsis,* His unveiling. At the present time, people may even deny that He exists but the time will come when all the world will see Him as He is, in the day of His power. (Morris p 201).

Those who do not know God and those who do not obey the gospel of our Lord Jesus will receive their punishment on that day. (2 Thessalonians 1:8). Paul describes them in Romans 1:28 as those who did not see fit to acknowledge God, (R.S.V; N.A.S.B.), did not like to retain God in their knowledge, (K.J.V.), or did not think that retaining the knowledge of God was worthwhile. Their punishment is severe, but merited. They will suffer eternal destruction and exclusion from the presence of the Lord and from the glory of His power when He comes to be glorified in His saints on that day. (2 Thessalonians 1:9, 10).

Eternal life belongs to those who have obeyed the gospel of our Lord Jesus. Eternal destruction will come upon those who have rejected the revelation which God has already given, the revelation of His Son. They have rejected His invitation to come to Him and acknowledge Him as Saviour and Lord, and in defiance of the offer of His grace, have separated themselves forever from the love that would have brought them to Himself.

Morris comments, 'the defiance of the will of God has eternal consequences, and separation from the Lord is the final disaster'. (Morris p 205).

It may seem strange that to suffer affliction and persecution for the sake of the gospel are accounted a privilege, and that those who suffer in this way are accounted worthy of the kingdom of God. (2 Thessalonians 1:5). But these are believers who have believed Paul's testimony, (2 Thessalonians 1:10,) who have been given the privilege of displaying and promoting God's righteous judgement through their suffering; of showing forth the God who also suffered; who sent His Son to be a propitiatory, expiatory sacrifice for our sins, not for the sins of the Thessalonians only, but for the sin of the whole world. (1 John 2:2). They suffer with Him and they will also be glorified with him. Or it could equally well be said, as they are suffering with Him now, they are being glorified with Him now. (Romans 8:17)

God sent His Son to live among men and women to demonstrate that relationship with God, fellowship with Him, was not only desirable but possible. Jesus taught men and women to call God 'Father'. (Matthew 6:9). And He provided for them new life, the abundant life which He wanted them to have (John 10:10), by giving up His life on the cross; not dying in a quiet room surrounded by His friends, but publicly, shamefully, displayed without dignity, on the cross of a common criminal. He had gone down into death taking sin with Him and destroying its power over men and women so that they could be free from sin and alive to God through our Lord Jesus Christ. (Romans 6:11).

God is righteous. Through His kindness, His grace, His mercy, He is leading and has led men and women to repentance, (Romans 2:4), to begin a new life of faith in Jesus. He is forbearing and patient with men and women, and to those who obey the truth He grants salvation, the forgiveness of their sin, new life in Him.

But there are some who do not obey the truth. Their hearts are hard and impenitent. (Romans 2:5). What can God do? He has given them the freedom of choice, the freedom to choose, and what they have chosen is condemnation for all their wickedness against God, their defiance of Him which has been building up in their lives as they wrest their independence from Him; as in the parable which Jesus told, they say, 'We will not have this Man to reign over us! (Luke 19:14).

This is why Paul can call God's judgement 'righteous', the righteous judgement of God. (2 Thessalonians 1:5). God cannot allow that wickedness should prosper. There has to be a time of reckoning, a time of judgement when the secrets of men's hearts will be revealed. (Romans 2:16).

There is only one solution. Such wickedness must be destroyed. Paul calls it eternal destruction. (2 Thessalonians 1:9). It has to be gone forever, eternally, never to be seen again, and to those who have participated in it, final. But an even more terrible judgement comes upon them, exclusion from the presence of the Lord and from the glory of His might, when He comes on that day to be glorified in His saints, and to be marvelled at in all who believed. (2 Thessalonians 1:9). They will never see His face again. They will never be part of the glorious unveiling of the Lord Jesus Christ when He comes in glory with His saints.

In his first letter to the Thessalonians, Paul spoke of the comfort of knowing that we shall be forever *with the Lord*. (1 Thessalonians 4:17). Now he says that those who have persecuted the church and 'have disobeyed the gospel of our Lord Jesus Christ' will be forever *without the Lord*. (2 Thessalonians 1:8).

Paul cannot imagine a worse destiny. The words of Moses to the people of Israel ring down through the centuries. 'I have set before you life and death.....therefore choose life, that you and your descendants may live'. (Deuteronomy 30:19). The judgement of God is never haphazard or capricious. It is absolutely righteous and depends largely on choices made by individuals, the calling of God upon their lives which they have ignored or rejected, or welcomed with grateful hearts as the answer to all their longings. But having made that choice, they discover that they had been chosen by God from before the foundation of the world. (Ephesians 1:4).This is the secret of predestination, of election.

The Thessalonian believers have responded to Paul's teaching, to his testimony. (2 Thessalonians 1:10). They are witnesses to Christ, even as Paul, Silas and Timothy are. The missionaries have every confidence that God would enable these believers to be worthy of the call upon them and that as they resolve to live by faith, and by every work of faith He gives them to do, the Name of the Lord will be glorified in them, according to the grace of God and the Lord Jesus Christ. And to this end, Paul, Silas and Timothy pray for them. (2 Thessalonians 1:11,12).

James is convinced that the prayer of faith will save the sick and this is an important part of praying for one another. (James 5:15). But the prayer of faith, believing in the power of the Lord Jesus and the advocacy of the Holy Spirit, (Romans 8:26), will also be effective in encouraging the weak, supporting the heavy burdened, and all who are in any trouble or adversity. Pray for another, says James. (James 5:16). Pray earnestly night and day, say Paul, Silas and Timothy. (1 Thessalonians 3:10). And when you stand praying, forgive, says the Lord Jesus. (Mark 11:25).

Leon Morris helpfully concludes that for believers, suffering is not optional, but inevitable. They are appointed to it. (1 Thessalonians 3:3).They must live their lives and develop their Christian character in a world dominated by non-Christian values, but their faith is not some fragile thing to be kept in a kind of spiritual cotton wool, insulated from all shocks. It is robust. The very troubles and afflictions which Christians endure are evidence that God is with them. (2 Thessalonians 1:5. Morris p 198).

Facing up to the gospel invitation, or turning away from it, is a choice fraught with the most solemn and lasting consequences. (Morris p 205). But in those who have believed in His name, His character, the reputation of Jesus is glorified. In that last great day, the glory of the Lord Jesus will be seen, not only because He Himself is glorious but His glory will also be seen in those who love Him, who have been redeemed by Him and are living in His grace. (2 Thessalonians 1:12). This is the prospect, the hope which Paul is declaring to his faithful, suffering brothers and sisters; and this why he prays for them. (2 Thessalonians 1:11).

Judgement of the unbelieving is necessary and will take place, but Paul's focus is on glory, the glory of Jesus and the glory to be found in the saints at the revelation of Jesus Christ, (2 Thessalonians 1:7), according to, and because of, the grace, the unmerited favour of our God, poured out upon His redeemed people through the Lord Jesus Christ.. (2 Thessalonians 2 :12). They may be encouraged that God is at work 'by His power', (2 Thessalonians 1:11), enabling them to be counted worthy to suffer for His sake, for the sake of the gospel; and 'by their faith in Christ', (2 Thessalonians 1:5), looking forward to the greatest fulfilment of their lives, with hope and expectation, knowing that He will be glorified and that by His grace they will have a share in that glory. (Wanamaker p 234).

2 Thessalonians Chapter 2

2 Thessalonians 2:1-2. Warning against false teachers.

Now concerning the coming of our Lord Jesus Christ and our assembling to meet Him, we beg you brethren not to be quickly shaken in mind or excited, either by spirit or word, or by letter purporting to be from us, to the effect that that the day of the Lord has come. Let no-one deceive you in any way. (2 Thessalonians 2:1-2).

There had been two issues troubling the Thessalonians which are here being dealt with by Paul. In his first letter, Paul had taken note of their suffering for the sake of the gospel, and here, in the second letter he had given them an explanation of the transforming work of the Holy Spirit in their sanctification which was was being accomplished through their suffering, for suffering was not without purpose, but would bring glory both to them and to their loving Lord.

In his first letter, Paul had also explained that the *parousia,* the second coming of the Lord, would be a glorious event, and comforted them concerning the status of those who had 'fallen asleep' when He came. But now, the glorious prospect of His coming again, which had been such a blessing to them as they struggled to keep going under their persecution, struggling to witness to His saving love 'in the midst of a crooked and perverse generation; (Philippians 2:15), holding forth the word of life', had been eroded by some who were saying that the day of the Lord had already come. How could He have come without their noticing it? Perhaps they had been negligent in watching and waiting for Him.

This is a new development in the community since Paul last wrote to them, Because of their strong belief in the Lord's coming and because they refused to renounce their faith, these believers have suffered severe persecution. But they have found comfort in the knowledge that God was with them and they can rest, be at peace, in His will. (2 Thessalonians 1:7).

But something worse than persecution has now arisen. There are deceivers, false teachers in Thessalonica who tell them that the day of the Lord has already come. These bruised and battered in spirit believers are now in crisis. If Paul could make a mistake about that, perhaps he could be wrong about other things he had taught them? Can they accept everything he says? Can all the promises of God *really* be for them?

Paul had more than adequately explained the coming of the Lord to them in his first letter, knowing the comfort that would give them, especially concerning their loved ones who had 'fallen asleep'. (1 Thessalonians 5:13,18), but also the hope that would give them as they suffered 'for His sake'. 'Jesus is coming soon', they would say to each other as they met to break bread. 'The Lord is coming soon! as they met to proclaim the Lord's death until He come.

Paul was not deceiving them. What he was sharing with them was the word of the Lord. He was declaring to the Thessalonians what God had shown to him and it was absolutely genuine. (1 Thessalonians 5:15).

Paul had explained to them about the 'times and the seasons', the 'now' and 'not yet', of the coming of the kingdom, (1 Thessalonians 5:1), that even the Lord Jesus Himself knew neither the day nor the hour when that appointed time would be fulfilled. (Matthew 24:36). Jesus was content to leave it in His Father's hands, trusting as He always did in His Father's perfect will. But He would surely come, like a thief in the night, when He was least expected. (1 Thessalonians 5:2).

But, the Thessalonians say, if He has already come as these people are saying to us, why did we not see Him? Why does everything continue just as it did before?

And it was not just that these deceivers were saying these things. They had produced a letter which they claimed had come from Paul, Silas and Timothy to the effect that the day of the Lord had come, (*enesteken*, (*Gk*) meaning 'is present', and not simply 'at hand' or imminent as in the KJV). Paul quickly disabused them concerning this letter. They know his handwriting, and can easily compare it with the letter he is writing to them 'with his own hand'. (2 Thessalonians 3:17), and may be seen in any letter he wrote. Paul says simply, 'it is the way I write'.

But he was fully concerned about their state of anxiety. They were 'shaken in mind', excited, disturbed. We beg you brethren, he says, listen carefully to what I say. (2 Thessalonians 2:1). These people may have tried to persuade you, not only by a letter purporting to come to you from us, but also by what you may have regarded as a Spirit inspired utterance, or even the spoken word. (2 Thessalonians 2:2). Do not be deceived by what they say, or by any method they may employ.

In the view of Bruce, there was probably no question that the teaching which the Thessalonians had received from Paul could possibly be superseded or replaced by an entirely different set of beliefs; but if they had heard such alternative teaching being proclaimed prophetically by someone claiming to have the gift of prophecy, they may well have been bewildered. (Bruce p 166).

2 Thessalonians 2:3-12. The great rebellion and the man of sin.

Now concerning the coming of our Lord Jesus Christ and our assembling together to meet Him, we beg you, brethren, not to be quickly shaken in mind or excited, either by spirit or word or by letter, purporting to be from us, to the effect that the day of the Lord has come. Let no one deceive you in any way for that day will not come unless the rebellion comes first and the man of lawlessness is revealed, the son of perdition, who opposes and exalts himself against every so called god or object of worship, so that he takes his seat in the temple of God, proclaiming himself to be God. (2 Thessalonians 2:1-4).

Paul's intention is to help these harassed believers by sharing with them further revelation about the coming of the Lord which he had received from the Holy Spirit. It is not impossible that he had also heard of the teaching of the Lord Jesus about His coming from his disciples Peter, John, and possibly Andrew who had been with Him in Jerusalem and heard Him speak, as He sat on the mount of Olives opposite the temple, (Mark 13:1-37; Luke 21:5-36; Matthew 24:3-57); though of course James the brother of John had later been killed by Herod, Acts 12:2).

Paul says that the day of the Lord's coming will not arrive until after 'the rebellion', which comes first, and then the man of lawlessness, the man of sin is revealed, the son of perdition who opposes and exalts himself against every god and object of worship, so that he takes his seat in the temple proclaiming himself to be God. (2 Thessalonians 2:3,4).

The believers had not misunderstood all that Paul had shown them before, of the necessity of waiting patiently for the day of the Lord that would surely come, and of waiting patiently with the appropriate behaviour of those who were expecting Him at any moment. It had become a powerful conviction with them that His coming would end their persecution, that a different world order would substitute for their present one, for they would be with their Lord in a completely different environment. They were confused, alarmed that they were now being told that the day of the Lord had already taken place, for they had not seen Him In glory and they were in exactly the same place regarding their lives as they had been before. They felt that this did not correspond with what Paul had told them.

How can Paul now help them to understand that that for which they were longing and waiting is still in the future? for they had believed and hoped that the gathering of the saints would soon include themselves, as part of the same last great cosmic event. (2 Thessalonians 2:1. Morris p 213).

Prophecy in the church is a gift of the Holy Spirit, a supernatural communication from the Lord, (1 Corinthians 12:9,11; 14:5,24-25, 31-39). This gift was a great joy to the believers, but they had apparently been listening to false prophecy, to prophets who were claiming the Spirit's authority but whose utterances were in fundamental opposition to what Paul had told them, and they wanted to know the truth. (2 Thessalonians 2:2). Jesus had warned that false prophets would come, (Matthew 7:15), and lead many astray, and that many would be deceived.

Paul gently gives them two reasons why, if they think that the Lord has already come, they are being deceived. 'Don't let anyone deceive you in any way, for that day will not come until the rebellion comes first, and then the man of lawlessness, the man of sin is revealed', says Paul, 'the man doomed to destruction'. (2 Thessalonians 2:3. Translation by L.Morris p 217).

Paul makes it clear that before the day of the Lord comes, there will be some truly memorable events. First, he says, there will be a vast rebellion of all the forces of evil against God, and secondly, there will be the appearance of a man whom he calls the man of lawlessness, who is also the son of perdition, meaning that he is destined for ignominy and final annulment. (2 Thessalonians 2:3).

Perhaps the Thessalonans were saying to Paul 'Why did you not tell us that before, Paul?' But he had said to them that when people say, 'there is peace and security', then sudden destruction will come upon them like the pains of childbirth on a woman in labour, and there will be no escape. (1 Thessalonians 5:3).

The peace and security appears to be evidence that all things continue as they have always been. People do not want change. Even if the present situation is not to their liking, it is what they know, what they have learned to deal with. Change is upsetting and stressful. It requires a new way of thinking, a new way of coping with altered circumstances. When there is no apparent change in the way the world works, this is what people would describe as 'peace and security'.

Paul reminded them in his first letter that there will be such a time, when people will be content to live in the present and not to consider the future; but the day of the Lord will come like a thief in the night, when sudden destruction will come upon those who live in the darkness of not knowing God, not belonging to Him. (1 Thessalonians 5:2-4).

Paul is anxious that his beloved brethren, his brothers and sisters, should be aware of the approach of that day, whatever the assessment of their present circumstances. They may be being deceived into believing that this is indeed a time of peace and security, or perhaps they suspect that they are about to witness sudden destruction. Paul goes on more minutely to speak of what the sudden destruction will consist.

As in many political as well as spiritual environments, there is a gradual build up before the explosive end, an accumulation of events preceding the final denouement. Paul goes on to speak of much that is hidden to normal view, deeply obscure to most human intelligence but alert to the eye of faith. He is now amplifying for the Thessalonians what it means; the end of peace and security, and the coming destruction before the great and terrible day of the Lord comes. (Acts 2:20).

When the Lord Jesus spoke of wars and rumours of wars, of nation rising against nation and kingdom against kingdom, and famines and earthquakes in various places, before the end comes, (Mark 13:7,8), this was not an altogether new concept to the disciples gathered round Him, listening to Him, for historically, had this not always been so? But as Jesus spoke they began to realize that there would be a definite, a definitive increase in world unrest before He came again.

Jesus went on to speak of climatic and ecological events in the natural world, earthquakes and famines in various places, an increase in these natural phenomena, an increase in these events which would enable those who are looking for His return to know that He is near, 'even at the doors'. (Mark 13:29. KJV). What a comfort, what an encouragement it is for His disciples when He says, 'heaven and earth may pass away, but My words will never pass away'. (Mark 13:31).

Jesus also wanted them to know of the increase in the persecution of believers throughout the world before His coming, but also increased activity in gospel preaching. (Mark 13:9,10). But then He speaks of something unmistakable and extraordinarily significant, the desolating sacrilege set up where it ought not to be. The gospel of Matthew adds to this by describing it as the desolating sacrilege which was spoken of by the prophet Daniel, standing in the holy place, initiating a time of great tribulation. (Matthew 24:15).

Is It possible to see in the desolating sacrilege, standing in the holy place, an identification with the person who is the man of lawlessness of 2 Thessalonians 2:3,4?

What has been described by the Lord Jesus echoes Daniel 11:36,37, where Antiochus Epiphanes is spoken of as profaning the temple and fortress, (meaning Zion), taking away the burnt offering from the altar and offering up a pig upon it which to the Jews is an unclean animal, the abomination which makes desolate. Daniel spoke prophetically.

We also read in 1 Maccabees 1:54 of the desolating sacrifice being erected on the altar of burnt offering, and in 1

Maccabees 1:21 of the desecration of the temple (by Antiochus Epiphanes IV, king of Syria, 175-163 B.C). Then, as now, some stood firm in their faith, those who fought for the restoration of the temple and for the freedom to worship their God; and those who today, unimportant and insignificant though they may appear to the outside world, are still rejoicing in the supreme acknowledgement that Jesus is Lord, and that He is all important to them, their Saviour and Redeemer.

But as in the time of the Maccabees, there would be some who violated the terms of their covenant with God. What happened under Antiochus could happen again. This is *apostasis, rebellion,* in the LXX or Greek version of the Hebrew scriptures. '*Apostasis*' originally meant political rebellion but came to mean religious rebellion after the events of the second century B.C. And of course has come into our language as apostasy, renunciation of faith in God, rebellion against Him.

Though 1 Maccabees is extracanonical, it was taken up by the Lord Jesus as He spoke of His coming again to His disciples, and this reference must therefore carry some validity. Prophecy is the proclamation of the eternal verities of the unchanging God. It may include a vision of God's present activity on behalf of His people; a prophet's concern with their daily life; or it may be the mysterious forth telling of the distant future. Jesus is of course speaking prophetically, but at the same time endorsing the prophetic utterances of the Hebrew scriptures.

But how do we understand the man of sin, the man of lawlessness, who has initiated this great rebellion against God? Who opposes and exalts himself against every so-called god or object of worship, so that he takes his seat in the temple of God, proclaiming himself to be God? (2 Thessalonians 2:4).

He has already promoted this great rebellion against God, the God who is in control, who rules everything, defying His authority and encouraging, perhaps violently forcing where he has the power to do so, defiance against God.

Paul speaks of *the rebellion, apostasia (Gk)* indicating a worldwide phenomenon of apostasy, even as Jesus had spoken of it in Matthew 24:10-12; the departure from God of so many of His elect, the falling away of many who had been led astray by false Christs and false prophets. (Matthew 24:28). Paul says the rebellion, the apostasy comes first, and then the man of sin is revealed, as though there had been a hidden under current going on all around which had made it possible for the man of sin to continue his work subversively for some time.

Isaiah has a telling phrase which could well apply to this period. He says 'darkness will cover the earth and deep darkness the people'. Darkness could accurately describe the apostasy, the rebellion against God which both the Lord Jesus and Paul saw was inevitable. But Isaaih does not stop there. He says 'but the glory of the Lord will rise upon you and His glory will be seen upon you!' (Isaiah 60:2).

As Isaiah was speaking prophetically, the deep darkness could apply equally to both the first and second coming of the Lord. It was certainly dark before He came down from His glory the first time. But before His second coming, there will be a time, an increase of darkness, an absence of meeting together in love, and faith, and truth; a famine not of bread and water, but a famine of hearing the word of the Lord. (Amos 8:11). But there will also come a time when the glory of the Lord will be revealed and all nations shall see it together, for the mouth of the Lord has spoken it. (Isaiah 40:5). And God will vanquish rebellion *apostasoi,* in the future, just as He has in the past. (Whiteley p 99).

Paul was certain that it would happen but did not know *when* it would occur, nor what form it would take. Whiteley says, 'Paul introduces it to show the believers that it is not yet'. (Whiteley, p 99). Paul calls it the mystery of lawlessness. (2 Thessalonians 2:7). Mystery in the New Testament normally refers to something previously hidden but which God has now revealed. This is the hidden lawlessness urged on by Satan, the adversary of God which will eventually result in the exposure of the lawless one for who he is. (2 Thessalonians 2:8).

Paul, as a trained rabbi (Acts 22:3), who had sat at the feet of Gamaliel, would have been familiar with the prophecies of Isaiah, Ezekiel and Daniel. To each of these devoted servants of His, God had given some expectation of what would happen at 'the time of the end', (Daniel 12:9); 'the appointed time'. (Daniel 11:29).

To Daniel and Ezekiel, these visions of the end time had come while the people of Israel were in Babylonian exile, far away from their homes, their temple and their beloved country. To Isaiah, the visions had come during the reigns of Uzziah, Jotham, Ahaz and Hezekiah, that is, from 769 B.C, (Uzziah), to 687 B.C. (Hezekiah), during which time Israel had suffered two crises of invasion; at the time of Ahaz, from Syria, (737 B.C; Isaiah 7), and at the time of Hezekiah, from Assyria; (Isaiah 36), as a result of not trusting the Lord. Isaiah pleaded with them to return to their relationship with their covenantal God. He describes the people as drawing near to the Lord with their mouth while their heart was far from Him and their fear, their reverence of Him as a commandment of men learned by rote. (Isaiah 29;13).

But Isaiah is full of hope for the future for he also sees One who is led as a Lamb to the slaughter and as a sheep that before her shearers is dumb, One who would be wounded for our transgressions and bruised for our iniquities, and by whose stripes we are healed, made whole, totally at peace with God. (Isaiah 53:5-7).

Though Ezekiel sees many dreadful visions of what the the end time will be like, he too sees a time when 'my servant David' a symbolic ancestor and 'type' or representative of the Lord Jesus shall be king over them, and God will make an everlasting covenant with them and set His sanctuary in the midst of them for evermore. (Ezekiel 37:24-28). These prophets both believed with all their being in the ultimate triumph of God.

The sanctuary, the dwelling place of God, was always an object of destruction and violence to those who opposed the worship of the God of Israel, worship of a different nature from that of the gods of the other nations. Daniel sees a future time, an appointed time when a contemptible person, to whom royal majesty has not been given, comes and takes action against the holy covenant, profaning the temple and taking away the continual burnt offering, setting up in its place the abomination which makes desolate. (Daniel 11:31).

And there shall be a time of trouble such has not been seen since there was a nation, till that time, but God's people will be delivered (Daniel 12:1), everyone whose name shall be found written in the Book, identified in Revelation 21:27 as the Lamb's book of life.

These men had mighty glimpses of the immediate future for their contemporaries, but also for the distant future, but Paul was able to contextualize their visions in the light of the life, death, resurrection, exaltation and coming again of the Lord Jesus Christ; the recognition that what the Lord's prophets had foreseen had not yet been fully realized by them, but that the future fulfilment of His word to them was to be the resounding triumph of all the ages, when He came in all His glory to take His people home to Himself.

Meanwhile, Paul had been given an insight into the compatibility of what the prophets of old had seen, and what was due to happen before that great and terrible day of the Lord came. As Daniel had foreseen, there will be a man of lawlessness, a man of sin, who was working towards worldwide dominion 'a contemptible person, who shall come in without warning and obtain the kingdom by flatteries'. (Daniel 11:21).

This is the one who will profane the temple and take away the continual burnt offering, and set up the abomination that makes desolate. (Daniel 11:31). This is the man of lawlessness, the man of sin who had been working towards the great rebellion of 2 Thessalonians 2:3, whose objective was world wide dominion which could only be adequately and sufficiently acknowledged when he sat in the temple of God proclaiming himself to be God, having opposed and condemned every so called god and object of worship. (2 Thessalonians 2:4). He wanted the worship for himself.

Whiteley comments, Israel had known many oppressors and many human 'saviours'. Now the people of God were to be faced with a worse oppressor than ever before, an oppressor who was the incarnation of Satan, the adversary of God. (2 Thessalonians 2:9). And this oppressor was to be overcome by the Son of God incarnate. (Whiteley p 100).

Just as Christ came by the power of God, so the man of lawlessness, the lawless one, will come by the activity of Satan, (Whiteley p 102). As he opposes God, he is an adversary of God, but Satan is the supreme adversary of God. Under his direction, being completely at the disposal of God's enemy, His adversary, who is the lawless one, will be given the ability, the power, to use signs and wonders 'with all wicked deception for those who are to perish, because they refused to love the truth and so be saved'. (2 Thessalonians 2:9). Therefore God sends upon them a strong delusion, to make them believe what is false, so that they may all be condemned who did not believe the truth but had pleasure in unrighteousness. (2 Thessalonians 2:11).

Jesus had warned that 'false Christs and false prophets will arise and show great signs and wonders, so as to lead astray, if possible even the elect'. (Matthew 24:24), and in his letters, the apostle John had assumed that his readers had heard that Antichrist was coming, although many antichrists were already active (1 John 2:18), and, John says, may be identified as those who do not confess that Jesus Christ has come in the flesh. (The heresy known as docetism. 1 John 4:2,3; 2 John 7).

Paul says to the Thessalonians, 'Do you not remember that when I was still with you I told you this? And you know what is restraining him now so that he may be revealed in his time'. (2 Thessalonians 2:5,6). Paul had explained to them that there would be 'times and seasons'.

We do not know when the Lord will take His power and reign, We do not know how long before He deals with all that militates against His reign. With the breath of his lips He could even now, at this very moment, 'smite the earth with the rod of His mouth in judgement, and with the breath of His lips slay the wicked', (Isaiah 11:14), and deal with all the wickedness and evil and iniquity in the world. But the iniquity of the wicked is not yet full. (cp Genesis 15:16). There will be a period of time when the man of sin is allowed full reign, but then comes a time when evil will be under the restraining power of God, until God regards it as appropriate to take His restraining power away, and the man of sin is 'out of the way'. (2 Thessalonians 2:7); until God's purposes are fulfilled and the lawless one is revealed whom the Lord Jesus will slay with the breath of his mouth and destroy him by His appearing and His coming. (2 Thessalonians 2:8).

It was inevitable and understandable that these believers were impatient for the coming of the Lord Jesus, when there was so much wrong that needed to be put right, and when they would see the Lord Jesus, the one whom they had come to love, given His rightful place. 'Be patient therefore until the coming of the Lord', counsels James echoing Paul and John. (James 5:7). Peter says, 'we know that there are some who say "where is the promise of His coming? for since the fathers fell asleep, all things have continued as they were from the beginning of creation". But Peter continues, the Lord is not slow concerning His promise, as some count slowness, but is forbearing towards you, not wishing that any should perish, but that all should come to repentance. (2 Peter 3:3,9).

Paul's encouragement to the Thessalonians lies in his determinative statement that the mystery of lawlessness which was previously hidden but now revealed, is always at work, but He who now restrains it will do so until the man of lawlessness is out of the way, for God, the Holy Spirit will have dealt with him. (2 Thessalonians 2:7). The lawless one will be strong, but the Holy Spirit's restraining power is greater.

Paul does not underestimate the activity of the lawless one. He attributes it to the activity and direction of Satan, the adversary of God who with his power and with pretended, false signs and wonders and with all wicked deception for those who are to perish, will delude men and women, But God is allowing them to believe a strong delusion, to make them believe what is false so that all may be condemned who did not believe in the truth when they had the opportunity, but had pleasure in unrighteousness. (2 Thessalonians 2:8-12).

God is *using* evil to forward His own purpose of love, for He is completely in control. (Whiteley p 103). And according to Romans 11:32, God has consigned all men to disobedience so that He might have mercy on all. He recognizes the disobedience in each one, so that He can have mercy on each one. 'O the depths of the riches and wisdom and knowledge of God! How unsearchable are His judgements, and His ways past finding out! (Romans 11:33). To Him be glory for ever'.

2 Thessalonians 2:13-17. Further prayer and thanksgiving.

But we are bound to give thanks to God always, for you, brethren beloved of the Lord, because God chose you in the beginning to be saved through sanctification by the Spirit and

belief in the truth. To this He called you through our gospel,
so that you may obtain the glory of our Lord Jesus Christ.
So then, brethren, stand firm and hold to the traditions which
you were taught by us, either by word of mouth or by letter.
(2 Thessalonians 2 :13-15).

Paul has said that 'that day will not come unless the rebellion comes first and the man of lawlessness is revealed'. (2 Thessalonians 2:3). Are the Thessalonians therefore disposed to spend their time looking for signs of the great rebellion? Longing as they are for the man of sin to be revealed and slain by the breath of the Lord Jesus so that the Lord Jesus should be glorified, take His power and reign?

It was important that the Thessalonians should understand about the end time, but more importantly that while waiting for the imminent return of their Lord, their lives should be an expression of their election, their calling, being chosen by God from the beginning to be saved. (2 Thessalonians 2:13). Paul calls them, 'brethren beloved of the Lord'. (2 Thessalonians 2:13). When he uses the word 'brethren', brothers and sisters, he is expressing his love for them. When he adds, 'beloved by the Lord', he is expressing an even greater truth, the love of the Lord for them. And so, the Lord's love for both him and them, and the love of the brethren for each other is a source of great comfort. Whatever may happen in the future before the Lord's return, He has promised never to leave them nor forsake them. They may rest in His promise.

They are His chosen ones. It was no accident that they had been 'called through the gospel'. (2 Thessalonians 2:14). In choosing to follow the call of the gospel, they were choosing what God had already chosen for them, for it was His intention, His will that through their belief, their faith, in the truth, and sanctification by the Holy Spirit, they might obtain the glory of our Lord Jesus Christ.

Paul is reiterating what he has said in his first letter, that as they have responded to Him, God has called them into a life worthy of God. He has called them into His own kingdom and glory. (1 Thessalonians 2:14). What a prospect for them! To share in the glory of the Lord Jesus Christ!

No wonder that in his *second* letter, Paul could not stop himself from giving thanks to God for them, *always*. (2 Thessalonians 2:13; 2 Thessalonians 1:2; and in his *first, constantly*, (1 Thessalonians 1:13). Thank you Lord, Paul is praying, that in spite of everything that is going to happen before You come, and when some of it may be happening already, there are those who look to You, who love You and love one another and who will stand firm in their faith, holding fast the traditions taught by me amd Silas and Timothy, by word and letter, as they eagerly look forward to Your coming again. (2 Thessalonians 2:15).

This is what he prays as he writes to his beloved brethren. We know that his grateful prayer of thanksgiving to God is heard. He had prayed that the Thessalonians should not be shaken quickly in mind, disturbed by those who would deceive them, saying that the *parousia*, the coming of the Lord, had already happened. He had prayed that they might not be deceived. His love and concern for them overflows in the absolute confidence he has, as he expresses it in prayer for them that the Lord Jesus Christ, the One who is coming, and God the Father, because of His love for them, will give them eternal comfort, encouragement and His grace.

Paul has by no means forgotten their circumstances, and this why he prays that they may know the presence of the Lord with them in the face of all the opposition which they are probably still encountering, that they may be encouraged to stand firm, without wavering, as the Lord continues to establish them in every good work and word, (2 Thessalonians 2:15-17), holding fast to the traditions taught to them.

These believers, young in the faith, had very little to hold onto but Paul, Silas and Timothy had given them 'traditions' (*paradosis*) to support them. Traditions are truth which having been received must be faithfully handed on. By tradition is meant the original teaching of the apostles, (Ephesians 2:20), not the ecclesiastical structure which all too soon was and is imposed upon it. (Stott p 178). By traditions, Paul meant the essential faith, the essential facts of the gospel which they had received, the life, death, resurrection and ascension of the Lord Jesus and what these facts conveyed to these hungry new believers, of life lived in the Spirit, just as He did, always committing Himself to the will of HIs Father, seeking always to please Him; daily, hourly in fellowship with Him.

These traditions were historical facts but were supplemented by, and included what was received from the Holy Spirit by faith. Paul states expressly in 1 Corinthians 11:23 that 'I received from the Lord what I also delivered to you' concerning the Lord's supper, a supper they enjoyed together, which had become a tradition as they remembered Him. And in I Corinthians 15:3,4, he says, 'I delivered to you what I also received', the salient facts of the gospel, received from the Holy Spirit through faith, that Christ died for our sins, according to the scriptures, and that He was buried, and that He was raised the third day according to the scriptures.

These traditions received from the Holy Spirit we hold in our hands as the sacred word of God, preserved for us in the New Testament, which the Thessalonians of course did not have. But they did have these letters sent by Paul, and they also had all that he had spoken to them while he was with them. And above all, they had the love of the Father. They had the grace of the Lord Jesus Christ. And they had the comfort and encouragement of the Holy Spirit. God would establish them in every good work and word. They were truly blessed.

Paul was confident that his prayer for his friends would be answered, for they had already been chosen by God, (2 Thessalonians 2:13), and the Holy Spirit, the Agent of sanctification, had already been fulfilling their desire to serve the living and true God and wait for His Son from heaven. (1 Thessalonians 1:9,10; 2 Thessalonians 2:13).

As Paul prayed for them, he confidently affirmed both for himself and them that the time would come when they shared the glory, *doxa, (Gk),* ineffable splendour, of the Lord Jesus. (2 Thessalonians 2:14). The Lord is already glorified in them because of their faith in Him and their love for Him and His beloved ones. How amazing it will be when He comes again and they will share His eternal glory, for as Paul told them in his first letter, 'then shall we be forever with the Lord'. (1 THessalonians 4:18).

This is what God has called them into, His own kingdom and glory so that the glory can be communicated to others, the light of *the glorious gospel of God* in the face of Jesus Christ. And so that others may be called out of darkness into His marvellous light as they see the glory in His face. (2 Corinthians 4:6; 1 Peter 2:9). There are many men and women still to come to Him, needing to hear the gospel so that they too may participate in the glory that will follow. (1 Peter 1:11. KJV). Denney says, 'from eternal choice to the sharing in the glory covers the whole work of God in creation'. (Quoted by Bruce p 192; and Stott p 175).

As Paul has prayed, so God has answered, establishing them in every good work and word, coming alongside by His Holy Spirit to give them encouragement and hope. (2 Thessalonians 2:16,17).

The gift of encouragement comes from the Lord and in spite of all that is envisaged in the last days before the *parousia*, the coming of the Lord, the Thessalonians are also given hope. It is not an empty hope, an optimistic expectation. It is founded upon the faithfulness of God to His word. KIngdoms may rise and fall, there may be earthquakes and famines in various places as the Lord Jesus had warned there would be, and these were but the beginning of sorrows. (Matthew 14: 8.) But the word of the Lord stands sure. The Lord knows those who are His. (2 Timothy 2:19). It is His seal upon them. It is a firm foundation upon which He and they are in agreement and at rest.

The fundamental eschatological hope is similar in both letters, but is expanded in 2 Thessalonians to meet an extraordinary challenge, (Karl P.Donfried p 110). But with the guidance of the Holy Spirit, opposed as it was to the false teaching among them, the Thessalonians will discover the truth, and will know what is the way of the Lord for them in their present situation.

2 Thessalonians Chapter 3

2 Thessalonians 3:1-5. The faithfulness of God.

Finally brethren, pray for us, that the word of the Lord may speed on and triumph as it did among you and that we may be delivered from wicked and evil men; for not all have faith. But the Lord is faithful; He will strengthen and guard you from evil. (2 Thessalonians 3:1-3).

As Paul prays for these precious Thessalonian believers, that the word of the Lord might speed on, and triumph, we are reminded of the words of the Lord Jesus, 'other sheep I have which are not of this fold. Them also I must bring and there will be one fold and one Shepherd'. (John 10:16).

The Thessalonian church is one of many even in Macedonia where something tremendous is taking place. The lost sheep are being found and brought into the fold, and this not only in Thessalonica but throughout Macedonia. And these new communities were not of Jews only but of both Jews and Greeks. Jesus had a great desire that all should hear His voice and follow Him so that he could give them eternal life, and being given eternal life by Him they could never perish, because they had been given to Him by His Father, and no-one is able to snatch them out of His Father's hand; His Father is God and greater than all. (John 10:27).

This is the core of Paul's ministry, to bring the word of God, in accordance with the great desire on the part of the Lord Jesus, to others 'not of this flock', 'not of this fold', that they may hear His voice and follow Him. Paul has been thanking God for the Thessalonians whom he loves. Now he is asking them to pray for him, for there are 'many other sheep', to whom he is preaching, many others who have not heard the voice of Jesus, who never had the opportunity of allowing the Holy Spirit to bring them encouragement and hope.

Paul is asking the Thessalonians to pray for him and Silas and Timothy who are at present in Corinth and from where the letters to the Thessalonians are being written. (Acts 18:5). It is more than possible that the Corinthian believers owed a great deal to the prayers of the believers in Thessalonica.

Paul asks them to pray that the word of the Lord might speed and triumph as he and his colleagues seek to establish the church in Corinth. In using the word 'triumph', Paul may have been thinking of a mighty chariot driving down the streets of Rome after a resounding victory over Rome's enemies. He uses the metaphor again in 2 Corinthians 2:14, when he writes, 'thanks be to God who always leads us in triumph and through us spreads the fragrance of the knowledge of Him everywhere'. The fragrance of the flowers that are thrown at the conquering armies as they parade down the streets cause Paul to pray earnestly that the fragrance, the aroma, the sweet smell of Christ may be spread both to those who are being saved and to those who are perishing. (2 Corinthians 2:14).

Paul, Silas and Timothy need the prayer of God's people so that they may not be accused of 'peddling' the word of God, using the gospel for their own profit and gain, (2 Corinthians 2:17), which seems ro be happening in Corinth at that time.

They also need their prayers 'so that they might be delivered from wicked and evil men, for not all have faith'. (2 Thessalonians 3:2). Paul knows from experience the effect of opposition on the preaching of the gospel; the suffering already experienced by so many ordinary believers as well as those privileged to be apostles, men who have been 'sent out' with the gospel, commissioned and anointed by the Holy Spirit for the work to which He has called them. (Acts 13:2).

Whether triumph or adversity, Paul knows that he can treat those two imposters just the same. Both could have the possibility of distorting the gospel, of deflecting the hearers from responding to the truth of the gospel.

How valuable then are the prayers of God's people; how absolutely vital their conviction that the Lord is faithful, (2 Thessalonians 3:3). Whether preaching or praying, this is the rock under their feet, that God is faithful; faithful to His word; faithful to His promises; absolutely trustworthy; pouring out His love and grace upon them as they pray in the Name of Jesus.

Paul recognizes that the ministry of prayer, meeting together at the throne of grace, (Hebrews 4:16), relies constantly on the faithfulness of God, for His knowledge is infinite, and all his beloved children want only to ally themselves with His will in everything. Yet there is also an added dimension in the lives lived by those who pray. Those who come to God *must believe* that He is, and that He is the rewarder of those who diligently seek Him. (Hebrews 11 :6). We come by faith, and can only come by faith.

But perhaps the most basic prayer of all is 'God be merciful to me, a sinner'.(Luke 18:13). We do not come in our own self righteousness. We come in His, relying on His mercy. We do not aspire to having reached some kind of moral perfection before we approach the throne of grace, for this is the place where we find mercy, and grace to help in time of need. (Hebrews 4:16). So in fear, that is, in reverence, in holy awe and sometimes with trembling, we come into the presence of a Holy God, knowing our weakness but knowing also His faithfulness, and as we pray, and as again we know and believe that the Lord graciously hears and answers our prayer, we affirm with confident assurance that 'the Lord is faithful'. (2 Thessalonians 3:3).

Paul also had confidence in the Lord about the Thessalonian believers, that they were doing, and would continue to do 'the things which we command'. (2 Thessalonians 3:4). Paul wants, even needs for them to 'pray for us', but his prayer for them is reciprocal. He prays that the Lord 'will direct their hearts into the love of God and the steadfastness of Christ', (2 Thessalonians 3:5), the arrow of the love of God and the steadfastness of Christ penetrating and piercing their hearts. What an amazing prayer, and what an amazing answer to prayer that would be!

This section of Paul's letter is introduced by the word 'finally'. Finally when all else fails, 'God is faithful'. Relying on the faithfulness of God, the Thessalonians are well able to deal with those among them who appear to be idle or contentious. (2 Thessalonians 3:6).

2 Thessalonians 3:6-15. Discipline in the church.

Now we command you brethren in the Name of our Lord Jesus Christ, that you keep away from any brother who is living in idleness and not in accord with the tradition that you received from us. (2 Thessalonians 3:6).

Paul is now speaking of the discipling of those believers who have misunderstood or who have in some way departed from the strict line of truth, the 'traditions' that they received from Paul, Silas and Timothy, as helping and encouraging them to be 'ordered'.

An alternative translation to 'living in idleness', is 'living disorderly'. (KJV). Paul has a strong objection to disorderly living by believers. He says in 1 Corinthians 14:40, that all things should be done decently and in order, not necessarily regulated, but ordered. Regulation speaks of an imposed discipline. Orderliness speaks of a desire of every individual in the church to give way to one another in love, while preserving all that has been given to them as directions from Paul and the other apostles, for they have been given to them by God through the

Holy Spirit. The apostles have been taught by the Holy Spirit that they might impart to the church the gifts bestowed on them by God, interpreting spiritual gifts to those who possess the Spirit. (1 Corinthians 2:12.13; 11:33).

But Paul is now laying down principles for them to follow. What he is doing is conveying to the believers what they need to hear, but not on his own authority but 'in the Name of our Lord Jesus Christ', (2 Thessalonians 3:6), on the authority of Jesus. Under the power of this authority, Paul can move steadily in his letter, from anticipation of the triumph of the word of the cross, as the gospel is preached, (2 Thessalonians 3:1); to the immense nature and privilege of prayer to a faithful God, (2 Thessalonians 3:3); to speaking of those in the church who are living in idleness and not in accord with the tradition which they had received from Paul; or 'from us' he says, including Silas and Timothy as being under that same authority and therefore of equal standing and influence as they ministered to the earliest believers in Thessalonica.

Paul has something to recommend to these believers who are living in idleness, walking disorderly, and not in accord with the traditions which they have received. Stott says that using the word tradition, *paradosis (Gk),* may indicate that Paul is referring to the teaching so recently given to them about the imminent coming of the Lord.

But Paul says, 'Look at us! You yourselves know how you ought to imitate us. (2 Thessalonians 3:7). We did not live in idleness while we were among you, waiting for the coming of the Lord. This was the example we gave you to follow. We did not behave disorderly among you'. (2 Thessalonians 3:7. KJV). It is possible that these believers had concluded that Jesus was coming soon, and that the whole world would be a different place, and with all that militated against God having been destroyed, it was no longer necessary for them to work. If anybody asked them what they were doing, they could say, 'we are waiting for Jesus'. It sounded so pious, to be waiting for the Lord's near return, and to spend time just waiting for Him and His glorification.

But how were they going to eat? How to provide for their families? They had been through a time of anxiety and bewilderment. At first, they had been excited at the prospect of the Lord's return. Along with others, they had turned from idols to the true God and to wait for His Son from heaven. (1 Thessalonians 1:9,10). Then they had been worried about their loved ones who had 'fallen asleep' and their destiny at the Lord's return, until reassured by Paul that we who are left, and alive, will be caught up together, raptured together with them to meet the Lord in the air. 'And so shall we be forever with the Lord'. (1 Thessalonians 4:17).

But then they had listened to false prophets who had told them that Jesus had already come. How could that be when they had been waiting so carefully for Him? Surely they would have seen Him? Then they had been told that although it was not in God's purpose that Jesus should come imminently, He would come after certain conditions had been fulfilled. At present, there was so much evil activity in the world, engineered by God' adversary, Satan, through a great rebellion or apostasy under someone called the man of sin, or the man of lawlessness. But restraint had been placed on this lawlessness by the Holy Spirit, a restraint entirely under His control or an even greater rebellion would have taken place.

The Lord Jeus could have dealt with this rebellion at any time, of day or night. But He is forbearing, not willing that any should perish, but that all should come to repentance and have eternal life. (2 Peter 3:9). But He is coming. There will be a glorification of the Lord Jesus when every eye shall see Him, including those who pierced Him, descending from the clouds with power and great glory. 'I am the Alpha and the Omega, says the Lord, who was, and is, *and is to come,* the Almighty'. (Revelation 1:7,8).

Some of the Thessalonians could only grasp one idea out of all this. Jesus has not yet come. But He is coming soon. And they say, we want to be ready for Him, waiting for Him. They know that they are the chosen of God, beloved of the Lord, and that they will be delivered from the wrath to come, (2 Thessalonians 2:13). But above all, they want to see Him glorified. Paul is saying to them, 'stand firm, remain strong, be loyal to all that you have heard about Jesus, His redemptive work, His teaching. (2 Thessalonians 2:15). Look to the encouragement you have in the Holy Spirit. (2 Thessalonians 2:16). And they are saying 'yes', to all that Paul says. But suppose they miss Him when He comes?

But Paul is saying 'yes' to them too.Yes, the Lord is coming, but He will not want to find us idle when He comes. We can spend time in prayer, for Paul prays for them constantly and is grateful when they pray for him and his colleagues. But prayer is what they can do at home, and as they go about their daily tasks, as well as when they have the joy of meeting together with others to pray.

Paul's work was preaching the gospel. While Paul was with them and ministering to them, was he not also waiting for the Lord to come from heaven? Paul remembered too how when he and Silas and Timothy had been with them, with toil and labour they had worked night and day so that they might not burden any of them. It was not because they did not have the right, but to give them an example in their conduct, for them to imitate. For even when they were with them, they gave them this commandment, 'if any man will not work, let him not eat'. (2 Thessalonians 3:10).

Paul affirms that those who preach the gospel have the right to live from the gospel, (1 Corinthians 9:14). Even those who served in the tabernacle were entitled to partake of the sacrificial offerings. (Deuteronomy 18:1).

Nevertheless, in Thessalonica, as in Corinth, Paul had not made use of this right, (1 Corinthians 9:12), in case it put an obstacle in the way of the gospel of Christ. He wanted to give no ammunition to those who may have thought that he made a profit from teaching, that he lived at the expense of those who had become believers.

If Paul and Silas and Timothy, therefore, were prepared to work to support themselves, then these beloved believers who had given up working, for whatever scruples or praiseworthy motive they might have had, were acting in a disorderly manner. They now knew that they had to imitate Paul in not living in idleness, for not only did not working cause them to be dependent on others, but it gave them time to be 'busybodies', (2 Thessalonians 3:11), 'prying into the private lives of others', as Bruce has it. (Bruce p 207). This had become a serious matter because the witness of the whole church could be compromised. To the outside world, it could appear that Christians are idlers, they do not work but they interfere in other people's lives.

Paul becomes very serious. He says, we command you and exhort you in the Lord Jesus Christ to do your own work in quietness and to earn your own living. (2 Thessalonians 3:12). Brethren, do not be weary in well doing; but keep going, persevere in doing good and keep looking for the day when Jesus will be glorified. And Paul continues, If there is anyone who has different ideas about what it means to wait for the Lord's coming, contrary to what he had written to them in this letter, have nothing to do with him. (2 Thessalonians 3:14). But he is still your brother. He is not your enemy and you must not treat him as such. But he is being disobedient and by leaving him to himself for a while, he may become ashamed and be restored to you. (2 Thessalonians 3:14).

Paul is adamant. He is as concerned for this wayward brother as he is for those who have stood firm in the teaching which he has given them. Do not look on him as an enemy but warn him as a brother, he says. When Christian discipline is necessary, it is to be given as brother to brother. It is not to be given in anger, still less in contempt. It is to be given in love. (Barclay p 253).

2 Thessalonians 3:16. Benediction.

Now may the Lord of peace Himself give you peace at all times and in all ways. The Lord be with you all. (2 Thessalonians 3:16).

Paul does not want his letter to the Thessalonians to end on a negative note.The Thessalonian believers have given Paul himself so much encouragement as their faith is growing abundantly and their love for one another is increasing, and they are remaining steadfast in the face of much affliction, much persecution which they are enduring. (2 Thessalonians 1:3).

So he prays these blessings over them. The first is the blessing of peace.The Lord is the Lord of peace. Where he is Lord there can be nothing but peace. It was what Jesus had spoken of to His disciples before He left them to go to the cross.'Peace I leave with you. My peace I give you. Let not your hearts be troubled, neither let them be afraid'. (John 14:27). This is the peace which we have in our hearts, that deep peace received from Him when we yield ourselves, our circumstances to Him unreservedly. This is what Paul wants for the Thessalonians, even for those who have so recently been disobedient, indeed, especially for them. But for them all as they continue to encounter opposition. Peace, the peace of the Lord Jesus.

The second blessing is of course concomitant with the first. Paul prays, 'the Lord be with you all', (2 Thessalonians 3:16). If we have the presence of the Lord with us; if we know that we are living in the presence of the Lord, then we are truly blessed.

At one time, in a state of anxiety about the future, Moses had said to the Lord, 'Show me your ways!' And the Lord had replied,

'My presence shall go with you and I will give you rest'. And Moses' response had been, 'If your presence go not with us, carry us not away from here'. Moses meant, away from this place where they had known and worshipped the Lord. (Exodus 33:12-16). The presence of the Lord alone could satisfy Moses as he led the people of the Lord through the desert, into the promised land.

Paul's blessing was also a prayer for them. Peace at all times and in every way; the presence of the Lord with them, all of them, all of the time; what more could the Thessalonians want or need? Bruce sees here an echo of the priestly prayer of Numbers 6:22. The Lord bless you and keep you. The Lord make His face to shine upon you and be gracious to you. The Lord lift up the light of His countenance upon you and give you peace. (Bruce p 212).

But the priest here is not Paul, but the HIgh Priest of our confession, Jesus. He is the one through whom we may have confidence to enter into the sanctuary, the holy place where He is, by the living way which He has consecrated for us, through the veil, that is His flesh, His Body. (Hebrews 8:12; 10:9). And when it comes to the presence of the Lord being with all of us, all the time, Bruce cannot help but remember the assurance, the promise, which Jesus gave His disciples, 'Lo, I am with you always, even unto the end of the age'. (Matthew 28:20; Bruce p 212).

2 Thessalonians 3:17-18. A final word.

I, Paul write this greeting with my own hand. This is the mark in every letter of mine; it is the way I write. The grace of the Lord Jesus Christ be with you all.

Paul's prayer for the blessing of peace and the presence of the Lord to come upon the Thessalonian believers had not quite been Paul's last word to them. He writes, 'I, Paul write this letter with my own hand, This is the mark in every letter of mine. It is the way I write'.

Paul recognizes that it is important, essential, for the Thessalonians to understand that the letter they are receiving is genuine, absolutely authentic. They had previously received a letter or letters which claimed that the coming of the Lord Jesus had already taken place, and what was even more to be deprecated, that the letters had come from Paul, Silas and Timothy, (2 Thessalonians 2:2).Paul wanted them to know that the letter which they were holding in their hands was genuine and there was no reason to suspect it, or speculate on its contents or to doubt its absolute veracity.

 Most commentators on this verse of 2 Thessalonians agree that Paul may have had an amanuensis, a scribe, to undertake the writing of the letter for him. This he had done later when writing to the Romans, employing a scribe called Tertius. (Romans 16:22). But it was especially important that the Thessalonians should have an example of Paul's own handwriting, in view of the deception with which those false teachers had tried to deceive them. So even if the majority of the letter had been dictated, the closing words were in his own hand, a hand which the Thessalonians recognized as 'the way I write'.

Paul really has come to the end of his letter at last. But he cannot help himself from adding one last benediction to these beloved, precious believers. And what greater benediction can he give them than 'the grace, the unmerited favour of our Lord Jesus Christ be with you all'. (2 Thessalonians 3:18). The overflowing grace of the Lord, His enabling, supporting power in action in their lives. This is his prayer for their blessing. We may be sure it was answered; grace from the Lord for them all. Paul begins and ends this letter to the Thessalonians with grace.

Select Bibliography

Bruce, F.F., *1 and 2 Thessalonians. Word Biblical Commentary,* (Word Incorporated, Waco, Texas, 1982)

Morris, Leon, *The First and Second Epistles to the Thessalonians (The New International Commentary on the New Testament),* (Wm. B Eerdmans Publishing Company, Michigan, 1991)

Stott, John, *1 and 2 Thessalonians: Living in the End Times (John Stott Bible Studies),* (Inter-Varsity Press,Nottingham, 1998)

Stott, John, *The Message of Thessalonians (The Bible Speaks Today),* (Inter-Varsity Press, Leicester, 1991)

Wanamaker, Charles A., *The Epistles to the Thessalonians. A Commentary on the Greek Text,* (William B. Eerdmans Publishing Company, Michigan; The Paternoster Press, Exeter, 1990)

Whitely, D.E.H., *Thessalonians in the Revised Standard Version,* (Oxford University Press, 1969)

Bible translation abbreviations:

K.J.V. : *King James Version* (also known as *The Authorised Version or A.V.*)

R.S.V. : *Revised Standard Version*

N.A.S.B. : *New American Standard Bible*

N.I.V. : New International Version

www.ingramcontent.com/pod-product-compliance
Lightning Source LLC
LaVergne TN
LVHW041225080426
835508LV00011B/1078